HOW TO CONTROL YOUR MONEY

REDUCE YOUR DEBT AND INCREASE YOUR SAVINGS

H. DOMINGUEZ

Q&A
Publishing

Published by
Q&A Publishing
25 Old Kings Hwy North # 13-280
Darien, CT 06820-4608

www.moneyconsiderations.com

Cover photo by Stephen Bayer.

ISBN 978-1-7329573-1-2

CONTENTS

DEDICATION AND ACKNOWLEDGEMENT

To my Parents.

Thanks to my wife Claudia for all her help to make this book a reality.

DISCLAIMER

The content of this book contains personal opinions of the author regarding financial and economic matters. It is for educational purposes only. Neither the author nor the publisher are engaged in rendering professional services including, but not limited to, accounting, tax, legal or investment planning. The information contained in this book is not intended as a substitute for such professional services, and if specific advice is needed or appropriate, the reader should seek out and engage a licensed professional.

The author and publisher expressly disclaim any liability, loss, or risks taken by readers who directly or indirectly act on this information. You are solely responsible for your own decisions and actions, and their results.

The fact that an individual, organization or website is referred to in this work as a citation or a potential source of further information, does not mean that the author or the publisher endorses the information they provide or recommendations they may make. Further, readers should be aware that websites listed in this work may have changed or disappeared between when this work was written and when it is read.

CONTENTS

PREFACE

Anyone paying attention to the news every day is aware that a lot of people are having problems managing their finances. According to a study conducted in 2015 in 148 countries by Standard and Poor's Ratings Services in partnership with other institutions, only 57% of Americans reach a passing grade in financial literacy (the ability to understand how money works in the world.)[1]

Even though few things other than your health can have a more significant effect on the quality of your life than your finances, how to manage your money was not a subject included in the education that most of us received when we were children, teenagers, and in many cases not even if we reached college. Unfortunately, for the most part, this continues to be the case nowadays. Therefore, most people still learn how to manage their money primarily by trial and error.

This book will show you in a brief, clear and I hope interesting way, how by understanding just a few fundamental concepts (less than ten!), you can manage and reduce your debt, control your spending, increase your savings, and get on your way to reaching your medium and long-term financial goals. You will learn the basics of how to take control of your finances.

The book has three main parts. In the first one, you will learn about the fundamental concepts that will give you the necessary framework to analyze all your money issues and understand their impact on your finances.

The second part focuses on the subject of debt. We will analyze its effect on your finances, when debt can be useful, and how to keep it within manageable levels. If like many people you are having some problems with your current level of debt, here you will find the steps you need to follow to reduce and take control of your debt.

In the third part, you will find not only what to do to keep your finances under control easily, but also to increase your net worth.

Also, to help you promptly put into practice the information presented here, you will find some simple and practical tools you can download for free, to start taking control of your money and improving your financial situation. So, don't waste any time (which really can cost you money), and start learning how to take control of your finances.

Good luck and I wish you success in your financial journey.

PART I

THE BASIC FRAMEWORK

1

THE MONEY QUADRANTS

When we observe our financial life from a macro perspective, it might seem not particularly complicated.

We all need or will need a series of goods and services. To pay for them, we must work to generate the necessary income. To buy some products we need, but that we cannot afford (like an unexpected expense or maybe a house), we can use credit (debt) and pay for them little by little during an extended period. Finally, we must save some of the income we generate while still able to work and invest it in assets that themselves can produce at least part of the income we will need in the future, when we will be unable or just won't want to work anymore.

However, despite that apparent simplicity, successfully managing our finances can be a challenge, if we don't have a clear framework to identify how every decision we make will affect our financial situation.

The most fundamental concept providing the necessary framework to understand your finances is the one we will refer to as the Money Quadrants. It is based on the idea that practically any financial activity we realize can be classified into one of four quadrants: income, expenses, assets, and debt. Everything you do that has an impact on your finances is part of one of those quadrants.

The Income Quadrant covers any money you receive from any source.

The Expenses Quadrant contains the money you use to pay for all the goods and services you buy, and any debts you pay.

In the Assets Quadrant, you will include all those assets you have acquired with the money you have saved, you created through intellectual or entrepreneurial endeavors, or that you have received or inherited.

Finally, the Debt Quadrant will include the money you owe to any person, company or organization, for any reason, and in any form.

2

THE INCOME QUADRANT

Let's analyze in some detail in the following sections, what are the key features and elements of each money quadrant.

Income Quadrant

As we mentioned before, in this quadrant we will include any money you receive, for any reason, and independently of the source. We will classify that money into any of three main categories of income, depending on the level of your involvement in the process of generating the income.

1. Active Income

This category will include any income you receive because of your work as an employee, independent professional or business owner. This kind of income is entirely dependent on your constant effort; the moment you stop working this income disappears. Here you should include any salary, bonuses, or professional fees received.

2. Passive Income

This type of income is generated and comes to you independently of any direct work on your part. Your involvement to be able to receive this income is limited to buying the financial instruments or acquiring or creating the non-financial assets on which you invest, and after that, you only have to perform those activities required for the effective management of those assets.

Here you will include any income you receive from your financial assets such as savings accounts, mutual funds, ETFs, individual stocks, and bonds.

Also any non-financial assets like royalties received for books, software programs, music, films or inventions, and rental properties. Alimony can be included here too.

When you retire, an essential part of your passive income will be represented by two main sources. First, your Social Security benefits and any pension you might be entitled to receive. Secondly, the withdrawals you make voluntarily or at some point required by law—when you reach 70 1/2 years—from some of your retirement accounts (such as IRA, SIMPLE IRA, SEP IRA, 401(k), profit-sharing, 403(b) or any other defined contribution plans). [1]

3. Aleatory Income

As its name indicates, this particular kind of income is completely aleatory, it might exist or not, and you never know whether you will receive it or when. It depends mostly on factors over which you have none or little control, such as winning a lottery or a raffle or receiving an inheritance.

During our life, we follow a progression through the different types of income that usually goes like this; as soon as you have your first remunerated job, you start generating active income. Later, when your career moves ahead and your income increases, you have more surplus money after covering all your expenses, which then you can invest in different assets with the expectation that they will appreciate with time.

By doing that, you start not only to generate passive income but also to gradually reduce the percentage that your active income represents of your total income. In fact, the basic idea behind retirement planning is to continue to do that systematically and efficiently, until your passive income reaches a point in which it can cover all your expenses, making you financially independent, and no longer requiring an active income. That's when working becomes optional.

Income Quadrant

I. Active Income

- Salary
- Professional Fees
- Bonuses

II. Passive Income

- Rental Income
- Royalties
- Alimony
- Financial Income:
  - Interests
  - Dividends
  - Capital Gains
  - Financial investments liquidation
- Retirement Income:
  - Social Security
  - Pension
  - Annuities
  - Retirement accounts distributions

III. Aleatory Income

- Lottery, raffles, etc.
- Inheritances

The Income Quadrant

3

THE EXPENSES QUADRANT

Your expenses can be classified into four categories:

1. Primary Expenses

Those that anyone in normal circumstances will have, such as housing, utilities, food, essential clothing, health products and services, transportation, and certain kinds of insurance you are required to have, like the one for your home (if you have a mortgage) and your car. These are your basic living expenses.

2. Secondary Expenses

These expenses can coincide with some of the same categories included within your primary expenses, but there is, however, an obvious difference, which is that secondary expenses cannot objectively be considered necessary or essential.

Examples of secondary expenses are a vacation home, gourmet food, luxury or fashionable clothing, a luxury, sport, or a second car, any insurance that you are not required by law to have, etc. These expenses are generated by things or services that are optional, and you can do without or at least limit them.

3. Debt Service

This category includes all payments you make of interest or capital to any debt you have (credit cards, student loans, car loans, mortgage, home equity loans and lines of credit, personal loans, etc.)

4. Aleatory Expenses

As the name implies, these are expenses over which you have no control, regarding when they can arise or what their cost could be. They are caused by accidents, sickness or any other unexpected situations, like when something breaks down. You can, however, limit their total cost, by buying insurance to cover some of those eventualities.

5. Savings

While not strictly an expense, savings need to be considered within this quadrant, because they should be a category in your budget. By doing so, you will transfer funds that are part of your income into your assets quadrant.

In most cases, it should be evident under which of these previous five categories any of your expenses fall.

Expenses Quadrant	
I. Primary Expenses	
- Housing	- Basic clothing
- Food (groceries)	- Transportation
- Utilities	- Phone
II. Secondary Expenses	
- Vacations	- Gifts
- Entertainment	- Hobbies
- Restaurants	
III. Debt Service	
- Credit cards	- Personal loans
- Taxes	- Mortgage
- Car loans	- Student loans
IV. Aleatory Expenses	
- Accidents	
- Sickness	
- Other unexpected expenses	
V. Savings	

The Expenses Quadrant

4

THE ASSETS QUADRANT

In this quadrant, you will classify your assets into five categories:

1. Financial Investments

These are represented by your saving accounts, CDs (certificates of deposit), mutual funds, ETFs (Exchange-Traded Funds), stocks, bonds, or any other financial instrument you can invest in.

2. Personal Property

Here you will include any property that unlike real estate is movable and has a significant value, such as vehicles (cars, trucks, SUVs, motorcycles, RVs, or ATVs.), fine jewelry, art (paintings, sculptures, etc.), antiques, and collectibles.

3. Real Estate Property

Here, you will include the equity you might have in your home or in any other real estate property you own, such as rental properties of any kind (residential, commercial or industrial.)

4. Business Equity

If you have your own business, here you will include any equity you have in it, based on the value of the company and your percentage of ownership. Determining the value of any business sometimes can be a little difficult, and obviously, it is a figure that will vary depending on the financial situation of the business, the conditions of the market, and the general economy at the time the valuation is done.

5. Intellectual Property

This category will include any intellectual creation you have that is protected by a patent, trademark or copyright, such as inventions, industrial designs, software programs and applications, books, films, or music.

Assets Quadrant	
I. Financial Investments	
- Savings account	- ETFs
- Certificates of deposit	- Stocks
- Mutual funds	- Bonds
II. Personal Property	
- Vehicles	- Art, antiques
- Jewelry	- Collectibles
III. Real Estate Property	
- Own house	
- Rental properties	
IV. Equity in Own Business	
V. Intellectual Property	
- Books	- Inventions
- Software	- Music

The Assets Quadrant

5

THE DEBT QUADRANT

Finally, within this quadrant, you will place any kind of debt you have: mortgages, car loans, credit cards, home equity lines of credit, personal loans, student loans, taxes, and judgment debt.

Debt can be classified in many ways depending on what aspect of it we focus on. Is something offered to guarantee the repayment of the loan? What's the type of interest rate applicable? What's the repayment term? Was a fixed amount of money lent by the lender or a credit line offered? What's the purpose of the loan? Who is the debtor or borrower?

It's important to know some of those classifications, because of the different rules affecting how each type of debt is treated.

Some of the most common ways to classify debt are:

Secured and Unsecured debt

Secured debt refers to a loan that is guaranteed by a collateral, which is something the lender can take in case the borrower doesn't comply with the payment terms of the loan or goes into bankruptcy or liquidation.

The collateral is an asset used to secure a loan, and the assets typically used as collateral are houses and cars. In these cases, the lender who lends you the money places what is known as a lien which is a legal recorded claim against your property, that will subsist until you repay your debt to that lender. A lien is usually a public record filed with the County Records Office when it applies to real estate property, or to some state agency like the Secretary of State for personal property such as cars, boats, etc.

Unsecured debt refers to that where the promise of repayment is not guaranteed neither by collateral (collateralized) nor by a guarantor (who is someone that promises to pay the loan in case the original borrower does not pay it back.)

Fixed or variable interest rate debt

This distinction is self-explanatory. If the same interest rate is maintained for the entire term of the loan, we will talk of fixed interest rate debt, like most of the mortgages. When the interest rate changes over the life of the loan, then we are talking of variable interest rate debt, and the typical example would be credit cards, or also some mortgages known as adjustable-rate mortgages (or ARMs.)

In this kind of loans, the interest rate that the borrower will effectively pay is determined by charging a spread or premium over an underlying interest rate or index, like the Prime Rate (the lowest rate of interest at which money may be borrowed commercially) or the LIBOR (London Interbank Offered Rate.) That spread will vary depending on the level of risk the lender is assuming, considering factors such as the kind of asset used as collateral and the credit rating of the borrower.

Fixed or variable repayment period

The first kind of debt is that which is set to be paid off by a specific date (like a mortgage for example). In debt with a variable repayment period, a date is not set for repayment, as in the case of credit cards.

Revolving debt

This kind of debt originates when a lender agrees to lend money to a borrower up to a certain maximum amount, on a recurring basis. The borrower can spend or use any amount below the maximum limit, and the periodic payment amounts (typically every month), will vary depending on the total amount the borrower has on loan at an agreed date.

Typical examples of revolving debt are a line of credit and credit cards. Revolving debt can be secured, such as in the case of a home equity line of credit, or unsecured like in the instance of a credit card.

Mortgages

These are loans specially made to purchase homes, and in which the real estate you acquire serves as collateral. In great part because of this, they usually have the lowest interest rate among consumer loans. Mortgages have a fixed payment term, usually 15 or 30 years, and as we have mentioned before, can have a fixed or a variable interest rate.

Installment debt

This type of debt refers to loans that should be repaid by the borrower in equal monthly payments (or installments), that include a portion of the principal owed plus the corresponding interest. This is the most common method of financing used to pay for high-priced items, such as home appliances, cars or houses.

Consumer, commercial, and public debt

These three types of debt depend primarily on who is the debtor: people or households, businesses, or governments respectively. Other differences also exist between these three types of debt, regarding aspects of their credit approval process, uses, and debt collection.

Consumer debt is the most important for the economy of the U.S. given that it represents around 80% of the nation's GDP (Gross Development Product, the value of all the goods and services produced by a country.[1]

According to the Federal Reserve Bank of New York, total household debt reached $12.96 trillion at the end of the third quarter of 2017, the highest it has been since the recession of 2008-2009, and the most important types of debt were: mortgages, student loans, car loans and credit cards.[2]

Debt Quadrant

- Mortgage
- Student loans
- Car loans
- Credit cards
- Home equity line of credit
- Personal loans
- Taxes
- Judgement debt

The Debt Quadrant

On the next page we will take a look now at all the money quadrants together.

Income Quadrant

I. Active Income
- Salary
- Professional Fees
- Bonuses

II. Passive Income
- Rental Income
- Royalties
- Alimony
- Financial Income:
  Interests
  Dividends
  Capital Gains
  Financial investments liquidation
- Retirement Income:
  Social Security
  Pension
  Annuities
  Retirement accounts distributions

III. Aleatory Income
- Lottery, raffles, etc.
- Inheritances

Expenses Quadrant

I. Primary Expenses
- Housing
- Food (groceries)
- Utilities
- Basic clothing
- Transportation
- Phone

II. Secondary Expenses
- Vacations
- Entertainment
- Restaurants
- Gifts
- Hobbies

III. Debt Service
- Credit cards
- Taxes
- Car loans
- Personal loans
- Mortgage
- Student loans

IV. Aleatory Expenses
- Accidents
- Sickness
- Other unexpected expenses

V. Savings

Assets Quadrant

I. Financial Investments
- Savings account
- Certificates of depo
- Mutual funds
- ETFs
- Stocks
- Bonds

II. Personal Property
- Vehicles
- Jewelry
- Art, antiques
- Collectibles

III. Real Estate Property
- Own house
- Rental properties

IV. Equity in Own Business

V. Intellectual Property
- Books
- Software
- Inventions
- Music

Debt Quadrant

- Mortgage
- Student loans
- Car loans
- Credit cards
- Home equity line of credit
- Personal loans
- Taxes
- Judgement debt

The Money Quadrants

Note. *- The samples of income, expenses, assets, and debts included in the different subcategories of each quadrant are not exhaustive.*

6

CASH FLOW

Now that you know the basics of the money quadrants, we can review two key concepts that result from the interaction between some of the quadrants.

First, we will review the concept of Cash Flow, which is based on the relation that exists between the Income and Expenses quadrants. Your cash flow represents the movement or flow of money that comes in as income from any source and then goes out when you pay for all your expenses.

Total Income Minus Total Expenses = Cash Flow

Many people confuse cash flow with a budget or vice versa or think they are the same tool. That is not the case.

A budget is a tool much more focused on planning. It provides a snapshot of how your finances would look for a particular period (a month, quarter, semester, or year) if your income and expenses follow what you established in that budget, and allows you to make sure the expenses you include are not higher than your income during that period.

The cash flow, on the other hand, is a vital instrument to monitor your liquidity. It is basically a measure of the extent to which you have enough money to meet all your financial obligations.

There are other fundamental differences between a budget and a cash flow report. In a budget, you always start from $0 and add your income and subtract your expenses to determine if the result for the period you are analyzing would be a surplus or a deficit.

On the other hand, when analyzing your cash flow, you always start with the balance you have on the date you begin evaluating your cash flow, in the checking account(s) to which you will deposit your income and issue all the checks or make the transfers required to pay for your expenses. You would then add or subtract, depending on the case, *when* income is received, or anything paid during the period considered in that cash flow. When are you going to receive the deposit for your payroll? When will you pay your rent or mortgage? And so on. With all this information you keep updating the balance of your checking account.

This gives you the opportunity, to see if the estimated timing of all the transactions will allow you to keep a positive balance during the whole period you are evaluating, or if you will need to delay some payment or payments or try to move forward some deposit.

Let me use an example to show you the clear difference between these two financial tools. Let's imagine that you have created a monthly budget for every month of the year. The numbers for next month show that you expect an income of $10,000, expenses in different categories for $8,000, and to contribute $1,000 to your emergencies fund and another $1,000 to your retirement savings account. So, looking at your budget, you know that as long as your income and expenses stay close to the numbers expected you should be fine.

However, when you review your cash flow, which allows you to monitor your checking account's balance for the same period, you immediately realize that you could have a problem (see table below).

Transaction	Date	Initial Balance: $200	
		Amount	Balance
Salary	06/01/18	$ 5,000	$ 5,200
Rent	06/02/18	$ (4,000)	$ 1,200
Food	06/04/18	$ (120)	$ 1,080
Restaurants	06/05/18	$ (250)	$ 830
Internet	06/09/18	$ (100)	$ 730
Credit Cards	06/10/18	$ (400)	$ 330
Phone	06/13/18	$ (100)	$ 230
Entertainment	06/13/18	$ (260)	$ (30)
Trip (Flight)	06/14/18	$ (500)	$ (530)
Salary	06/15/18	$ 5,000	$ 4,470
Cleaners	06/16/18	$ (150)	$ 4,320
Car	06/17/18	$ (500)	$ 3,820
Food	06/17/18	$ (130)	$ 3,690
Credit Cards	06/18/18	$ (300)	$ 3,390
Insurance	06/21/18	$ (100)	$ 3,290
Emergency Fund	06/22/18	$ (1,000)	$ 2,290
Restaurants	06/22/18	$ (250)	$ 2,040
Entertainment	06/23/18	$ (240)	$ 1,800
Trip (Expenses)	06/27/18	$ (300)	$ 1,500
Savings	06/29/18	$ (1,000)	$ 500

Negative balance shown by cash flow report.

Your income will be represented by two deposits for a total of $5,000 made by your employer on the 1st and the 15th of the month, but you had estimated to pay bills during the first ten days of the month for $5,730. That would put your balance in the red for $530.

After reviewing the expenses you expect to have, you notice that you can make a few changes to solve your cash flow problem. You can postpone buying some things (like the flight for a trip you have planned) and reduce what you spend in restaurants during the first half of the month. By doing those changes, you will be able to keep a positive balance in your checking account during the whole month and avoid overdraft fees and/or bounced checks.

As you can see, while your budget allows you to prioritize your spending and saving goals and keep them within your income and the parameters you want, you also need to monitor your cash flow, to make sure you always have enough funds to cover all your bills. The conclusion to remember here is that, even if you make and follow a budget, you can have problems to pay your bills on time if you don't also monitor your cash flow.

Your Cash Flow Balance

At the end of any period you consider in a cash flow report, you can end up with any of three possible results that will have very different implications for your finances.

1. Balanced Cash Flow (Income = Expenses)

This would be the result of your income and expenses being precisely equal for that period, something that doesn't happen very often.

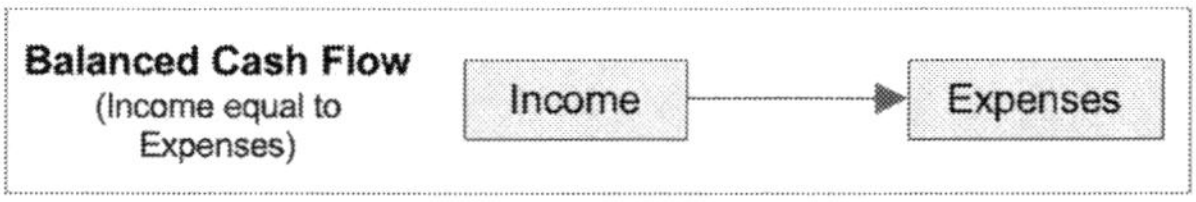

It might seem that having a balanced cash flow puts your finances in a somewhat neutral position (and obviously is much better than having a negative cash flow). In reality, it can be a precarious situation, especially if you don't have some money saved, that can be used to cover any unexpected expenses, which inevitably sooner or later you will have to pay (like those caused by repairs, accidents, or sickness).

2. Negative Cash Flow (Expenses > Income)

This results when you have more expenses than income and puts you in a difficult situation because you will need to look for ways to cover or manage the deficit.

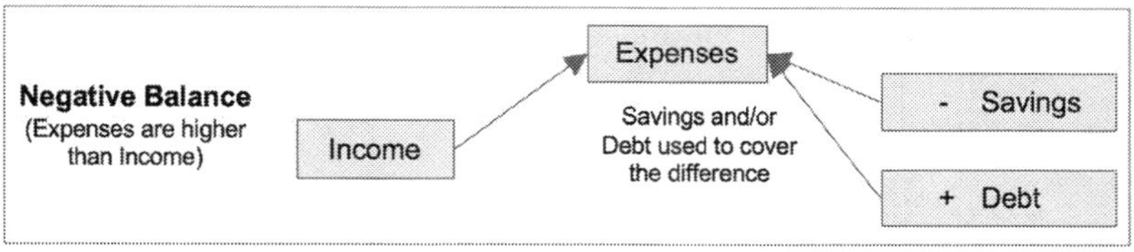

Some options are:

1. On the rare occasions when the negative balance is caused by a delay in receiving some income, postponing the payment of some expenses (if possible), may be enough to eliminate the negative balance in a subsequent period. If that's not an option, another alternative could be to pay for some of those expenses with a credit card and then pay the card as soon as you receive the income you were expecting to avoid having to pay any interests.
2. Use some of your assets, such as withdrawing money from your savings account or selling some financial investment (mutual funds, stocks, bonds, etc.) to pay for

some expenses. Of these two options, using resources from a savings account should be preferred, if possible, because selling stocks, mutual funds, bonds or ETFs that have experienced some gains will cause you to owe the corresponding taxes.

3. Use some of your assets to cover part of the difference between your income and expenses and incur some debt to pay for the balance (by using one of your credit cards, for example.)
4. Cover all the difference between your income and expenses by incurring in debt (by using a credit card, the money you get by applying for a personal loan, or from an already approved home equity line of credit among other possible alternatives).

These options are listed from the one that would have a minor or no adverse impact on your personal finances (1), to the one with the most negative consequences (4).

If you go for option 1, you may have to pay some fees for late payment, and probably suffer some adverse effect on your credit score.

Option 2 would decrease your assets, but hopefully, you could start repairing that damage very soon.

Option 3 would create a more long lasting problem, by negatively affecting two of your money quadrants. First, you would increase your debt, not only in the amount you borrow to cover part of your income deficit but also with the interest generated by this debt until you fully pay it. Additionally, you would decrease your assets in the amount used to cover the balance of your income deficit not covered by the new debt you incur.

Option 4 in many cases could be the worst because the payments you would have to do to repay the total amount of money borrowed plus interest, would increase your expenses for future periods, making it even harder for you to reach a balanced or positive balance cash flow anytime soon.

3. Positive Cash Flow (Income > Expenses)

When your income is higher than your expenses, you have a positive cash flow. You have the opportunity to grow your assets quadrant by investing that income surplus in different kinds of assets (financial investments, real estate, or business equity), allowing you to start looking for ways to diversify your sources of income.

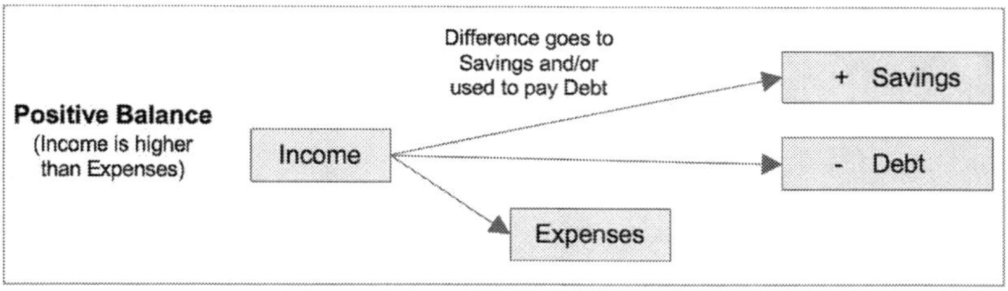

7

MANAGING YOUR CASH FLOW

If you want to keep your personal finances under control and healthy, you need to start budgeting your expenses and managing your cash flow.

There are several ways to budget your expenses. One way is by using a spreadsheet. You first make a complete list of all your sources of income, how much revenue you estimate to receive from each source and when, and if it will be recurrent income, with what frequency you will receive it (monthly, biweekly, once a quarter, once a year, only once, etc.) Then, you must create another list containing all your expenses, also including when you will have to pay for them and with what frequency.

If using a spreadsheet is an option you might feel comfortable with, you can download a template I prepared to create an annual budget and review your cash flow, that you can start using immediately. You can modify it in any way you wish to satisfy your needs. To download the template go to my website at: moneyconsiderations.com/tools/

An even better option to make a budget and manage your cash

flow, because of many additional features available, would be to use any of the multiple programs specifically designed to handle personal finances. These programs might require a little longer learning curve, but will give you much more flexibility to explore different options in your cash flow, and many other useful features.

Some of the most popular are Mint, Personal Capital (both free and web-based), Quicken, Moneydance (available for Mac and Windows), and Banktivity (Mac).

It is a good idea to budget and plan your cash flow for at least three to six months in advance, no matter which tool you use. Going for a more extended period usually is not worth the effort, because there will always be unexpected circumstances from time to time that will force you to change your numbers.

Once you are in the habit of keeping a budget and monitoring your cash flow, you will notice that having a clearer view of how your cash flow will behave in the coming weeks and months will reduce your stress substantially. Even if the numbers you see are not the ones you would like, you will feel more in control of your finances.

Besides, by getting into the habit of continually monitoring your cash flow, you will be more in sync with the importance of looking always for ways to increase your income and reduce your expenses, not just keeping them under control.

8

NET WORTH

We have seen so far two essential concepts to understand and manage your finances: the money quadrants and cash flow. The third fundamental concept that everyone who wants to have healthy finances needs to understand is the concept of net worth.

We saw before how the concept of cash flow is based on the relation between our Income and our Expenses. The concept of net worth depends on the connection between the other two quadrants, our Assets and Debts.

The net worth of a person, business, or any other kind of organization is calculated by subtracting from total assets the total amount of debt. So, your net worth is the value of all your assets minus the total amount of debt you owe. This concept of net worth is the one that tells us how much wealth a person has, how much that person is worth from a financial point of view.

Total Assets Minus Total Debt = Net Worth

There is a definite difference in the way you measure your cash flow and your net worth. The determination of your cash flow is a little more dynamic because you will always determine it after considering all your income and expenses during a specified period, normally a month, quarter, semester or year. So, you will say that your cash flow was positive, balanced, or negative for April, the second quarter of last year, or is expected to be for this year.

On the other hand, the calculation of your net worth is more static, given that you calculate how much was the value of your assets minus your debt on a specific date, like December 31st of a particular year for example.

While the formula to determine your net worth is simple, calculating the value of some of your assets might not be so easy. In part for this reason and also because the most valuable assets for the majority of people are primarily represented by financial and real estate assets, in many cases, they consider just the value of those two assets as their net worth.

You shouldn't have much trouble determining the exact value of all or most of your financial assets. You just have to get the corresponding statements from the financial company or companies where you have your accounts.

For your real estate property, you will have to rely on some of the same methods realtors use to determine the value of the property, such as comparing it with similar properties in your area that have been recently sold or maybe even with those that are for sale for a known price.[1]

You can get that kind of information from websites like Zillow.com, Trulia.com or Realtor.com. Once you have determined the property value, if you have a mortgage on it, don't forget to subtract the amount you still owe to your lender on the date you are calculating the net worth to determine how much is your equity.

Trying to assign a value to your personal and intellectual property can be a little more difficult and not as precise. In the case of your personal property, usually you can determine the approximate value for your property based on information gathered from websites, magazines or catalogs specialized in the kind of asset you want to value.

To determine the value of cars and other vehicles you might have (motorcycles, RVs, etc.), you should find the price at which similar vehicles have been recently sold in your area.

If you own some antiques, or any piece of art and you don't have a relatively recent valuation done by an expert, try to estimate their value based on the best information you can find about comparable pieces.

Finally, if you own any intellectual property such as copyrights or patents, the process you will have to follow to determine its value requires a little more work on your part, and you might only be able to put an estimated value on those assets you already commercialized and are currently generating income for you.

Importance of Tracking Your Net Worth

Focusing your attention and efforts on increasing your net worth is the only way you can achieve someday financial independence. For this reason, calculating your net worth at least annually should be part of your financial planning. It will help you assess your progress and determine how close you are to reaching your financial goals. It can also make you aware of needed adjustments or changes in the way you are managing your finances.

In the end, your net worth is a very objective indicator of how well you have handled all the income you have generated during your life. Have you been able to keep a good part, or have you spent most of it?

Like in the case of your cash flow, you can keep track of your net worth by using a spreadsheet, or any of the most popular programs to manage personal finances mentioned before when talking about cash flow. If you feel comfortable with or prefer to use a spreadsheet, you can download a template I created, that might save you some time and effort, and use it as a starting point to create your own. To download the template go to: moneyconsiderations.com/tools/

The Risk of Confusing High Income with Wealth

Many people wrongly believe that having a high level of income is what makes you rich, or at least a precondition to becoming wealthy. However, a lot of people have a good level of income or even a very high-income, but given that they also have high expenses, sometimes even higher than their earnings, their net worth can be surprisingly small. Because of this, the standard of living for people in that situation can very soon be at risk, if for any reason their income were to diminish even just for a brief period.

This is why it is not unusual to read about artists, athletes, and even some entrepreneurs, who when they go through situations where for any reason their income decreases or disappears even temporarily, tend to experience severe financial problems.

Always remember that while having a high income can be of great help to increase your net worth, multiple studies have found that the key factors to accumulate a considerable net worth and become financially self-sufficient are your spending and saving habits.[2]

Two Very Important Cycles

There are two critical cycles that not only show the links between your cash flow and net worth, but that can also produce totally opposite results in your finances.

The Active Income Replacement Cycle

First, we will refer to the cycle we will call the Active Income Replacement Cycle (AIRC). This cycle forms when you have and maintain a positive cash flow, and instead of spending the part of your income that exceeds your expenses, you transfer it to your assets quadrant by investing it in different assets that will later produce passive income. When you do this, little by little that passive income will reduce the percentage that your active income represents from your total income, while at the same time you increase your total assets. To magnify these two positive results and multiply this cycle's power, one of the best strategies you can follow is to reinvest any passive income you receive, into the same assets that generated such revenue, or in other kinds of assets that could produce even higher income.

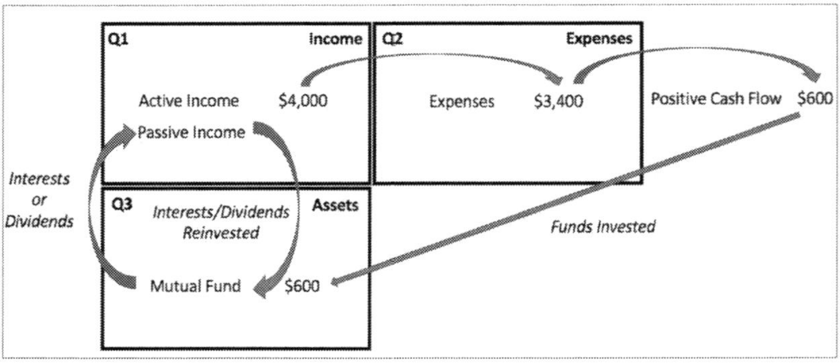

How the Active Income Replacement Cycle Works

If you do your best to keep the AIRC going, you will reach a point where your passive income by itself, or later on together with your retirement income, are enough to cover all your expenses without requiring any active income. That will give you the independence of no longer needing the security of a full-time job, making it possible for you to retire or do something else.

Some people don't seem to grasp how vital this is, but if for some reason you are not successful in replacing your active income with some form of passive income by the time you would like to retire, your only options will be:

- Postpone your retirement and keep working until you can replace your active income (if ever); or
- Retire anyway, but reducing your standard of living to be able to get by with the amount of passive income you have.

Another important benefit generated by the active income replacement cycle is that by growing your total assets, it will contribute to increasing your net worth.

The Debt Creation Cycle (DCC)

This other cycle represents the exact opposite of the income replacement cycle. It starts when you have a negative cash flow for a relatively extended period, until you reach a point where you don't have any assets that can be used to cover the deficit between your income and expenses. Then your only available option is to acquire more and more debt.

If you are in that kind of situation and you don't find a way to increase your income or reduce your expenses substantially, you will reach a point where you are no longer able to get access to any more credit given the amount of debt you have already accumulated. At that point, you will be unable to cover your expenses, which have increased now by the interest accrued.

If you cannot negotiate with your creditors a restructuring of the debt in terms that make it payable with your current income, the last option could be to declare bankruptcy. However, this option should be considered only as a last resort, because as we will see later, it is not just complicated and relatively expensive but can stay on your credit report for up to 10 years.

One of the best ways to avoid falling into the Debt Creation Cycle (DCC) is by doing your best to estimate and manage your future cash flows. That will give you time to take steps to keep your expenses below your income. You will know when you need to look for ways to increase your income or postpone secondary expenses to avoid having a negative cash flow. If you cannot avoid it, you can at least try to reduce having a negative cash flow as much as possible, to make it a little more manageable.

Let's see how this cycle works with a straightforward example.

Imagine a man who has a monthly income of $4,000 and expenses of $4,200. As you can see in the chart below, of those $4,200 in expenses, $3,700 correspond to primary expenses (necessities like housing, food, clothing, and in most cases transportation), and $500 to secondary expenses (for categories like entertainment, vacations, or better ways to satisfy necessities). To cover the $200 deficit in his income, this person decides to use a credit card to pay for some expenses, which only postpones having to face the problem.

The next month just to avoid increasing his debt, even more, this guy would have to reduce his expenses by more than $200 just to have a balanced cash flow. That's because now he needs also to start paying his new debt (at least the interests accrued, but hopefully also part of the capital owed.) Such a reduction would probably have to come from secondary expenses that usually are easier to eliminate than to lower basic expenses. If the reduction was let's say of $225 ($200 less to keep his expenses and income in line, plus a minimum credit card payment of $25), it would represent a 45% reduction over his secondary expenses during the previous month ($500). That would be a significant reduction. Besides, this person's credit card balance probably would stay very close to its initial amount for quite some time, until he can make a more significant payment toward the capital owed.

On the next page you will see a graphic showing the effect of the debt creation cycle.

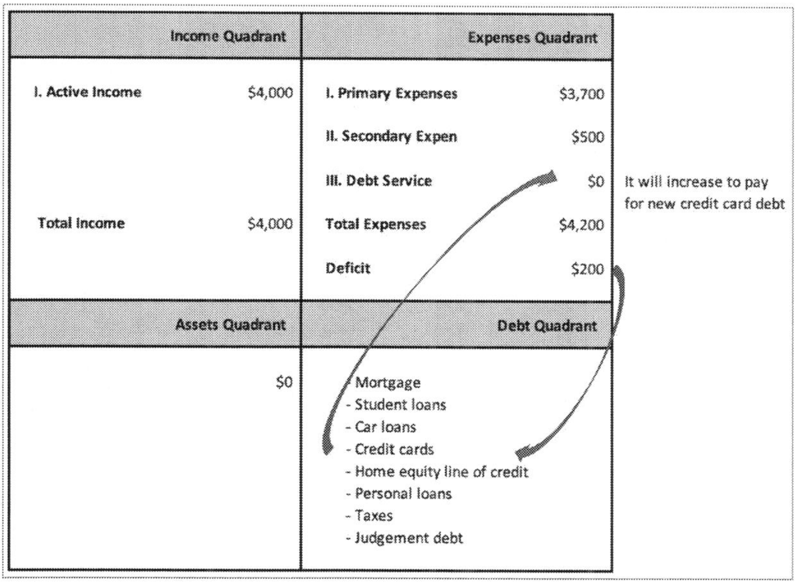

How the Debt Creation Cycle Works

As you can see, while the active income replacement cycle helps you increase your net worth, the debt creation cycle can decrease it very fast and cause severe damage to your finances.

PART II

UNDERSTANDING DEBT

9

DEBT

Debt seems to be an always present topic of discussion and analysis everywhere: in newspapers, magazines, books, TV and radio programs, podcasts, blogs, newsletters, social networks, etc. However, the concept of debt is not one that many of us could succinctly define if someone were to ask us: what is debt?

From a practical point of view, we could say that in its purest form, debt is a way or means to make it possible to buy things we cannot afford.

One of the multiple problems involving debt is that when most people think about debt, they do it independently of its correlative concept of credit. But we need to keep in mind that any debt always implies a relationship between two parts. Debt is created when one party receives credit or money, provided by another party. Any of these parties can be a person, an institution, organization, or even a country.

The party providing the credit or money is usually identified as the creditor or lender. The side which receives the credit or money is called the debtor or borrower. Most of the time, the debtor, and the lender enter into a contract where they specify the terms and conditions under which the debt will be paid.

The role and the position of lenders and borrowers have changed through times as the general attitude toward debt has evolved. If you are interested in knowing a little more about this evolution, there's a very brief history of credit and debt in Appendix A of this book.

The most important and essential conditions of debt are the term for repayment and the amount of interest rate. The term for repayment is the period the debtor has to repay the total amount of the debt, which includes the amount of credit or money received, also known as the principal, plus any agreed interest. The interest rate is the fee that is charged by the lender to the debtor or borrower, for the ability to use the credit or money he or she receives.

Types of Interest Rates

The interest is usually established as a percentage of the principal, calculated monthly or annually, and can be fixed or variable (meaning that it depends on an underlying interest rate or index.) In loans with a variable interest rate, the underlying interest rate or index usually depends on the type of loan.

So for example, in the case of auto loans, credit cards, and some mortgages known as adjustable-rate mortgages (or ARMs), the underlying benchmark rate usually is the prime rate. The prime rate is the interest rate commercial banks charge to their most credit-worthy customers, who typically are large corporations.

In this kind of loans, lenders—usually banks and financial institutions—charge some percentage points over the benchmark rate. This is known as the "spread." So, the effective rate the borrower will have to pay is set as "prime rate + X%." The size of the spread will depend on various factors, such as the type of asset used as collateral and the credit rating of the borrower.

Some Factors Influencing Interest Rates

Some other elements that are considered by lenders to determine the kind and amount of interest they charge to borrowers, besides the forces of supply and demand are:

- The opportunity cost for the lender, which means the cost represented by the lender's inability to use for anything else the money that is being lent out.
- The expected inflation during the term of the loan. The lender will try to make sure the interest rate charged to the borrower considers the expected rate of inflation so that the amount repaid by the borrower considering principal and interest is equivalent to the one originally agreed to in real terms (after inflation).
- The length of time the money is lent out, due to the possibility of economic or political circumstances that might affect interest rates and inflation.
- The level of liquidity of the loan, meaning how easy it would be for the lender to sell his rights during the term of the loan.

Is All Debt Bad?

We have already seen the problems that can arise when you don't keep your expenses at least in balance with your income and use debt to cover such imbalance. Does that mean that you should avoid debt at all cost? Well, not really.

While there is no unanimity about when debt can be considered good and when bad, there's consensus that in general, good debt helps you increase your net worth by allowing you to buy an asset that will increase its value or make it possible for you to generate long-term income. Any other kind of debt is normally considered bad.

The basic rule to avoid having bad debts is simple: *if you can't afford it* (and if you have to use credit to buy it that's probably the case), *and you don't need it, don't buy it.* Debt is something that has to be handled with extreme caution if we don't want to cause severe damage to our finances.

There are however at least four cases in which incurring debt (paying for something using credit) could make good sense:

First Case

> The first will be if you are going to buy a high-cost asset that will keep or maybe even increase its net value with time (that is after considering the effect of inflation.) Probably the clearest example of this is buying a house.
>
> Most people buy their home using a mortgage loan because they don't have enough money to pay for its total price, but only a percentage of it represented by the down payment they make. Then they finance the balance for a term of 15 or 30 years, making it affordable to pay for it. If you buy a house located in a good area and pay a reasonable price, chances are high that it will keep its value in the future and probably even increase it in net terms (after inflation.) All this can make buying a house using a mortgage loan a financially sound strategy.
>
> This approach doesn't make much financial sense, despite

being widely used, to acquire other high-priced assets whose market value depreciates fast, like for example a new car. In this case, the moment you leave the dealership your car's value is already around 10% less than what you paid for it.

Even worse, most cars lose around 50 to 60% of their value in the first five years. The only valid exception might be when you need a car because of your job, and if that's the case, probably buying a recent model used car would make much more financial sense, because then you wouldn't suffer the impact of the high depreciation mentioned before.

Second Case

The second case would be when you use credit to pay for a service that will improve you, making it possible to increase your income in the future. For example, when you finance the cost of college, post-graduate studies or any kind of education or training that will improve your professional qualifications.

You have to keep in mind, however, that there has to be a reasonable correlation between the cost of such education, and what you can realistically expect to earn once you conclude your studies. Incurring a debt of $200,000 to study for a profession in which very few people earn more than $50,000 per year doesn't make much financial sense.

Third Case

> A third case can be when "new debt" is generated as part of a debt consolidation strategy, carefully designed to reduce the total cost of your debt and bring it under control.

Fourth Case

> Finally, the fourth case would be one where going into debt might not really be an option, but the only possible way to pay for medical services that are required. We are talking here of any case in which you or some family member might need some unexpected and expensive medical treatment, beyond what your medical insurance and your emergency funds might be able to cover.

A strategy that could make sense, but only for some people, would be to use very short-term debt to buy things you could pay cash, just to get some benefit offered by a credit card. The typical case would be to use a credit card that offers you a certain percentage of cash-back, miles, or points you can use to pay for other things and services you need. This could be like getting a small discount just for using a credit card to pay for things that in any case you would buy and could pay cash.

However, this strategy only works if:

1. You pay your full credit card balance when it is due to avoid having to pay any interest; and,
2. When the amount of the benefits you receive (cash-back,

miles, points, etc.) is higher than any annual fees, you might have to pay for the credit card.

The requirement mentioned in the point 1 above is precisely why this kind of strategy doesn't work for most people. According to a report by the Federal Reserve, only 45 percent of all credit card holders pay off their full balance every month.[1] If you are part of this group and choose the right credit cards to pay, you can be in effect saving money.

10

WHY DO MANY PEOPLE OVERSPEND?

To the question, why do some people have so much debt? the first almost automatic answer is because they overspend, and available figures seem to support that answer.

Data from the Bureau of Labor Statistics released as part of their 2015 Consumer Expenditures Survey, show that a little over 38% of all households have had expenditures that exceeded their disposable income (gross income minus taxes).[1] Other entities and organizations analyzing this same subject reach different numbers but agree with their general conclusions.

For example, research done by FINRA (the Financial Industry Regulatory Authority, Inc.) in its Investor Education Foundation's Financial Capability in the United States 2016 report, found that only 40% of Americans spend less than their income. Of the other 60%, nearly 40% spend their full income, and the rest spend more than their earnings.[2]

So, despite the differences in numbers, the conclusion is that there's an incredible amount of people overspending in this country, even when everyone knows (probably except for the government), that if you spend more than what you make for an extended period, you will end up having financial troubles. Then the question is why do we do it?

Factors that Contribute to People's Overspending

Many circumstances and factors can play a role in people overspending, but among the most common are (in no particular order):

- Medical costs
- Inflation
- High-interest rates
- Lack of insurance
- Identity theft
- An expanding family
- Divorce
- Poor investments
- A reduction in income
- Underemployment
- Gambling
- Little or no savings at all
- Easy credit
- Not having a budget

If we analyze all these and many others factors we could have mentioned, it becomes apparent that we could divide them into three main groups.

1. Unexpected Situations

This first group would include those few situations that are entirely random, and no one can know if, or when, they can present in our lives. Here we would include cases such as a sudden disease or medical emergency, identity theft, sudden unemployment or underemployment, or the death of the breadwinner of the household.

2. Lack of Financial Knowledge

In a second group, we can put all those situations that to a significant degree can be considered a consequence of a lack of financial knowledge. Among these would be, for example, not knowing how to create a budget and monitor your cash flow; not being able to determine the best kind of loans or investments for your particular situation; or not knowing what financial decisions can negatively affect your credit score and why.

3. Lack of Personal Discipline

Finally, in this third group, we can place all those situations that are merely the result of our own shortcomings. Here we should include things such as:

- Gambling;
- Banking on an "expected" windfall;
- Applying for easy credit—but that we know is expensive;
- Buying things that you want but don't need and cannot afford, just to keep appearances;
- Not being willing to adjust your expenses when for any reason your income goes down.

Sometimes we buy into the myth that we are what we own, and then it seems we never have enough stuff or the right kind. As we accumulate things, we feel more powerful, confident and successful (at least for a while), until we realize that we didn't need all that, and even worse, we can't even afford it.

The Importance of Improving Your Financial Literacy

After considering all the situations included in the three groups mentioned above, you can very quickly conclude that improving your financial knowledge is one of the most important things you can do.

By increasing your financial knowledge, not only you will be able to deal in a much more effective way with the many unexpected and stressful situations that sooner or later you might face, so that they don't cause profound or permanent damage to your finances. You will also make better decisions in general, on all those things that can have a meaningful impact on your personal finances. Things such as renting, buying or selling real estate, determining when and how to use credit effectively, getting insurance, creating and using a budget, paying for college, investing, or tax and retirement planning.

A lot of people don't have the right level of financial knowledge, not because they have a particularly difficult time understanding financial concepts. Usually, it is because no one taught them the most essential and basic economic concepts that would allow them to have healthy personal finances. Nor their parents, and neither their teachers.

According to the National Financial Educators Council, just 17 states require students to take a high school course in personal finance, and only 20% of teachers feel competent to teach it. This could be the most critical deficiency of our educational system, given the impact the lack of financial knowledge has in everybody's quality of life. It's difficult to believe that less than half of the states require economics classes in school, and even fewer require personal finance classes.

Finding ways to help people overcome some problems like low

self-esteem or lack of discipline is the challenging part. It doesn't matter how much financial knowledge people can have if, in the end, they are not willing to do what they know is the right thing for their finances.

11

HOW MUCH DEBT IS TOO MUCH?

How Much Do Americans Owe?

As mentioned before when discussing the Debt Quadrant, total consumer debt including mortgages was $12.96 trillion at the end of September 2017. It has been growing, reflecting in part the improvement of the economy since the last recession, but also showing some changes, like for example people postponing home purchases and instead borrowing more to buy cars or pay for college. Mortgages continue to represent the largest part of overall consumer debt (67.4%). However, student (10.5%) and auto loans (9.3%) have increased their participation of the total.

An interesting analysis done by NerdWallet, based on data from the Federal Reserve Bank of New York and the U.S. Census Bureau among other sources[1], shows the totals owed by an average U.S. household (that carries that kind of debt) at June 2018:

Type of debt	Total owed by average U.S. household (1)	Total debt owed by U.S. consumers
Credit cards	$15,482	$927 billion
Mortgages	$181,176	$9 trillion
Auto loans	$27,669	$1.24 trillion
Student loans	$46,950	$1.41 trillion
Any type of debt	$134,058	$13.29 trillion

Debt balances are current as of June 2018

(1) Carrying this type of debt

American households were using on average 9.8% of their disposable income (income left after taxes have been paid) on debt service at the end of the second quarter of 2018, according to figures published by the Federal Reserve.

How does your current situation compare to the amounts mentioned above for the most common types of consumer debt?

Do You Owe Too Much?

There are different ways to evaluate your debt level. The first step, if you have not done it yet, should be to determine exactly how much are your current income and total debts.

Then, one of the easiest ways to calculate your debt load is to figure out your *debt-to-income ratio*. You determine this ratio, by just comparing your monthly debt payments to your monthly income. Let's say you earn $5,000 a month, and between your mortgage (or rent), credit cards, auto and student loans you pay $1,350 every month. Just divide the $1,350 by the $5,000 (= 0.27) and multiply the result by 100 to come up with a percentage, in this case, 27%. That's your debt-to-income ratio, and it's typically considered that you should try to keep it at 36% or lower. A ratio that is lower than 30% is excellent, but one over 40% indicates that your finances could experience a severe crisis.

You can also calculate your debt-to-income ratio but only consider the amount you spend each month on what's referred to as the bad debt, such as credit cards and personal loans. This will allow you to know what it is called your *debt overload*. A bad debt ratio higher than 10% is considered too high and indicates that you are overloaded with debt.

There are many subtle indications (and some not so subtle), that should be considered as a warning that you have too much debt. Among them:

- You have fallen into the habit of just paying the minimum amount due on your credit cards every month.
- Sometimes you juggle payments, delaying payment to one company to be able to pay another.
- The credit limit on any of your cards has been reached.
- It is becoming more and more difficult for you to pay ordinary expenses (like rent, mortgage, or groceries.)
- With some regularity, you are spending more than what you earn.
- You are unable to save, even small amounts, to keep a fund that could help you confront any contingency like having to repair your car or any appliance, a pay cut or a period of unemployment.
- You have received more than one late payment notice from any of your lenders.

Some rules of thumb to help you keep the most common kinds of consumer debt at manageable levels are:

- Housing - Limit housing costs to 25% or less of your net

income (which is your total income from any source, after taxes and any other deduction).

- Car loans - Keep your monthly car payments between 5 and 10% of your net income. Make a down payment of 20% and take loans for a term of four or fewer years so you won't stay for many years owing more than what the car is worth.
- Student Loans - Try not to borrow to pay for a degree, more than what you can realistically expect to make your first year out of school. The Wall Street Journal reported last April that according to figures from the Federal Reserve of New York, 5% of student-loan borrowers owe more than $100,000, but they account for almost a third of all outstanding student debt.

Now, don't forget that while rules of thumb can be a useful guide, they don't take into consideration the characteristics and situation of any individual person, so you should not completely rely on them to keep you out of financial troubles.

12

HOW TO TAKE CONTROL OF YOUR DEBT

Let's say you have decided that it is time to take control of your debt, how do you do it? Follow the next steps.

1. Stop increasing your debt by using cash

When so much of your money is being used to pay your creditors, that you have a hard time covering your basic needs with what's left, the first step toward putting your finances in order is to stop adding debt. For many people, the quickest and most efficient way to curb their spending is to become a cash-only consumer. Credit and debit cards can make it too easy to overspend. Many people can keep their expenses more easily under control when they adhere to a policy of paying with cash for groceries, clothing, vacations and anything else, other than their rent or mortgage and car loan.

2. Make a budget

It is something that probably you have avoided, but now you

must create a budget. A budget is a fundamental tool to make sure you are making the most of every dollar you earn, and to help you reach your financial goals. In essence, it's just a financial plan that allocates specific amounts of money to be spent on certain things. However, you can also use a budget to lower your overall debt by following these steps:

- First list all your fixed monthly expenses, such as rent or mortgage, utilities, and car payments.
- Next, list all your variable expenses, those that change from month to month like groceries, gas, entertainment, etc. Use your credit card or bank statements to make sure you include all.
- Now determine how much exactly is your monthly net or disposable income (gross income minus taxes).
- Next, subtract the value of your fixed and variable expenses from your disposable income. What's left is how much you could spend on lowering your debt. If you have been relying on credit cards to expand your spending capacity, you might be surprised at how small this amount is, or you may even find it is actually negative. You can increase it by looking for items from the variable expenses that you could eliminate, or at least reduce.
- Now make a list of all your debts, including their balance, interest rate, and minimum payment required. Sort it by interest rate, from the highest to the smallest.
- Add all the minimum payments you have to make and subtract that amount from the amount you already determined you can use to lower your debt. The difference is what you can use to start paying off and eliminating your debt.

No matter how much debt you have, a healthy habit that can have a very positive impact on your finances is to review periodically all your variable expenses (at least every six months) and look for all those you could reduce or eliminate. If unfortunately, your current debt has gotten so out of control that your income barely allows you to cover your required minimum payments, then you should do this review right now.

Sometimes even the most disciplined among us, let his or her guard down and buy something or subscribe to a service that we shouldn't have. So, go ahead and sell all that stuff and cancel all those services you don't use or need. For things or services you need, look for ways to substitute them for equally good or even better versions, but less expensive. This effort to reduce your expenses can produce excellent results and don't forget also to think about possible ways to improve the other side of your financial equation, your income.

3. Choose the Best Method to Reduce Your Debts

After you have reached this point, you will have to pause and make some decisions about what kind of strategy could be more useful for you, regarding how to use the amount of money you have available to pay your debt once you cover all your required minimum payments. There are two main and very different strategies or methods you can use to liquidate your debt. One is known as the snowball method and the other as the ladder method.

The Snowball or the Ladder Method?

The snowball method looks to generate momentum by focusing on the size of your balances, and basically works like this. You pay at least the minimum amount due on all of your credit cards, and then use the rest of the money you have available to lower your debt, to pay the credit card or any other debt with the smallest balance. Repeat this process every month, so you pay off that card's balance as quickly as possible. Once you do it, move to the next credit card with now the smallest balance and repeat the whole process.

The ladder method focuses instead on reducing the total amount of interest you will have to pay until you can liquidate your entire debt.

To accomplish this, you pay the minimum amount due on all of your credit cards and use your available money to lower your debt to pay the credit card that is charging you the highest interest rate. You do this every month until you pay off entirely that card's balance. Then you move down a rung of the ladder and use all your available funds after paying the minimum amounts due on the rest of the cards, to pay the card that is now charging the highest interest rate. Repeat this process until you finish paying all your debt.

Keep in mind that the interest rate you have to pay determines how fast your debt will grow and how much more you will have to pay every month. The ladder method minimizes the amount of interest you pay, which means you will end up paying less overall.

There's something you should know about these two methods. Obviously, from a purely financial point of view, the ladder method is the best, given that it saves you the most money over the long term by focusing its efforts on eliminating first the balances on the accounts that are charging the highest interest rates.

However, in some cases, it might take a while to close an individual account in full. For this reason, this method usually works better for people who are good with long-term planning and accepting delayed satisfaction, who normally are not the majority of those facing a debt problem. So, if you are the kind of person that expects fast results or gets frustrated easily, this method might not be the best for you.

On the other hand, for many people the snowball method can be the most effective way, from a psychological point of view, to accomplish the goal of eliminating their debt problem. Its focus on the accounts with the smallest balances makes it possible to pay off their debt relatively fast, and each account you take to a zero balance becomes a milestone reached, which can be very rewarding and keep you motivated in your efforts to liquidate your debts.

In fact, research conducted by the University of Michigan and recently highlighted in the Harvard Business Review, concluded that people focused on paying down the account with the smallest balance experience a more potent effect on their sense of progress, and consequently, in their motivation to keep paying down their debts.[1]

4. Consolidate your debt

There's another strategy you should carefully consider, no matter which of the two methods mentioned before you will use to pay and liquidate your debts, and that strategy is debt consolidation.

Debt consolidation is a form of debt refinancing, by using a new loan to pay off multiple existing debts on more favorable terms. You can use it to transfer all or some of your current debts into one single debt at a lower interest rate, which will allow you to reduce the total cost of your debt.

To successfully consolidate your debts, you should find an unsecured loan or credit with the best terms and conditions available to you. As you may remember from what we mentioned in a previous chapter, unsecured loans are those based only on your promise to pay and are not secured by any asset or property that could be foreclosed or repossessed by the lender to pay the loan, such as a house or car.

Unsecured loans usually have higher interest rates than secured loans because they are riskier for the lender, and you can find it more difficult (or impossible) to be approved for them if your credit score is too low. However, consolidating unsecured debts into a secured loan is not considered wise. You could lose the asset securing the loan if for any circumstance you fail to pay in the agreed terms.

Besides the main benefit of reducing the cost of your debt, consolidation can also offer some other benefits, like making the management process of your debt easier, by having to track and deal with fewer transactions. This can be an important benefit, considering the average American cardholder has seven credit cards.

When someone is experiencing money problems, just deciding how much money to pay for each card can represent a difficult and stressful juggling act. Also, when managing multiple credit cards, you increase the possibilities of missing a minimum payment which would result in penalties and fees.

Keep in mind that just because you are thinking of using the snowball method to liquidate your debts, doesn't mean you cannot also go ahead and do some debt consolidation. You don't need to consolidate all your current debts. You could consolidate only some of them, at least the ones with the highest interest rates so that you reduce the total cost of the interest your debt will generate until you can pay it off completely.

Options for Debt Consolidation

Depending on a good measure on your current credit score, there might be different options you can explore to do an efficient debt consolidation.

A. Transfer Balances to Credit Cards with a Lower Interest Rate

One of the best options for consolidation can be to use a new credit card offering a 0% or a low introductory APR (annual percentage rate) during a period, that in some cases can be of twelve or more months. Most card issuers already include the option to transfer balances during the application process. They usually charge a fee for such transfers, which recently has been around 3% of the transferred amount.

Once the transfer has been made, you should try your best to pay it during the promotional period to avoid interests altogether or pay only the lower interest rate offered, which would represent significant savings.

B. Use a Home Equity Loan

If you own a home and have some equity because you put a decent amount of money as a down payment, plus the increase of that equity through the years as you paid off part of the mortgage, you might consider getting a home equity line of credit (HEL) for the maximum amount possible.

Because an HEL is a secured loan (your house would be the guarantee of your payment) it is, as we mentioned before, a riskier option, but has a much lower interest rate (around 5%) than credit cards (about 15% on January 2018). So, by using the funds from the HEL to pay off your cards, you will save a good amount of interest.

C. Borrow from family or friends

Borrowing money from your family or friends might be a good option if you are comfortable with the idea. You could offer to pay them an interest rate that is better than what they are receiving for money they have in their bank, but substantially lower than the rates you are paying on your credit cards. This would make it attractive for the person lending you the money and also for you.

To avoid any misunderstandings or hard feelings that might affect the relationship, use a written agreement establishing the interest and the repayment schedule, and more importantly, adhere to it.

D. Borrow from your 401(k)

This option can be a little more complicated and risky than the others mentioned before, but worth considering in some cases as another alternative to reduce the cost of your debt. First, you must check with your 401(k) plan administrator whether your plan gives you the option to borrow against your account balance. That's not always the case.

If your plan allows it, before borrowing from your 401(k) you need to evaluate the advantages and disadvantages carefully.

Let's start with the positives.

- The interest rate you will have to pay is usually much lower than what credit cards charge. It's normally set based on the Prime Rate, plus 1 or 2 percentage points. The Prime Rate is published every day by the Wall Street Journal, based on surveys of 30 bank's lending rates (currently it is at 4.5%).
- Another positive characteristic is that, given the nature

of the 401(k), you will pay back not only the loan principal but also the interest to yourself, and not to the financial institution that manages the plan. The totality of the loan repayment has to go back to your 401(k) account.

- If you request a 401(k) "loan," no credit check will be performed, given that technically you are not borrowing money from anyone, but tapping temporarily into your retirement funds. So, this could be a good option for people who would have problems getting credit at affordable interest rates, like when their credit score has been damaged because they have filed for bankruptcy in the recent past or had to make a short sale of their house. Additionally, borrowing from your 401(k) does not have any impact on your credit rating.
- Usually, any application fees are minimal. Many of the plans charge a small origination fee (typically under $100 per loan) that goes to the administrator of the plan.

On the other hand, these are some possible disadvantages of borrowing against your 401(k).

- There are limits to the amount you can borrow. If you participate in a 401(k) retirement plan at work, very likely you will have the option to borrow only up to 50% of the account's value or $50,000, whichever is smaller. If your account value is less than $20,000, there is usually an exception that allows you to borrow up to $10,000, even if this is your entire balance.
- If the funds you borrow are used for debt consolidation (or for any other reason other than buying a house), you must repay them in five years or fewer.
- While contributions to your 401(k) plan are made with pre-tax dollars, if you borrow from your plan, you need

to pay with after-tax dollars, which means that your take-home pay will be reduced by the amount you pay. Because of this, it is a good idea to consider what your projected income would be during that period, and make sure you can manage with the estimated take-home pay after the deduction of the payments on a 401(k) loan. It's important also to know that, if for any reason you don't make a payment for 90 days, the borrowed money will be considered a distribution and taxed as income, plus a 10% penalty if you are younger than 59 and a half years old.

- Another essential aspect to take into consideration is your job stability because the terms of 401(k) loans are tied to your employment status with the employer offering the plan.
- Until 2017, when you ceased working for your current employer for any reason before you repay in full the loan, the outstanding balance became due, and generally, you were required to repay it within 60 days. However, recent changes to the tax law now give until the due date for filing your tax return (which means until April 15 of the following year or October 1st. if you file for an extension) to repay the loan balance. Otherwise, the loan balance will be taxed as a distribution.
- You should keep all this in mind when considering the convenience of borrowing funds from your 401(k), given that even if you are happy with your employer and vice versa and you are not aware of the possibility of any layoffs, if your job ends, things could get complicated.

For all these aspects, some financial advisors insist that borrowing from your 401(k) should only be considered by those who cannot have access to a home equity loan or cannot borrow from a family member, and just when they are in a desperate situation.

E. Borrow against a life insurance

Depending on what type of life insurance you have, you might have the option of borrowing from it. While originally life insurance was designed to pay a sum of money (death benefit) to a beneficiary in the event of the insured person's death, some insurance products evolved to incorporate savings or investments. Now, because of those changes, if you have permanent life insurance with a cash value, such as whole life insurance or a universal life insurance policy, it may be possible for you to borrow against it.

Review your policy to see if it includes a loan provision. Also, contact your insurance representative to check if your life insurance has built a cash value, and if so how much is it. Discuss with him or her what process you would have to follow to get a loan, the impact to your policy, and the possible tax implications.

Your insurance agent will have to run what's called an "in-force illustration" to show you how your loan would impact your insurance policy.

Many people have the misconception that when you get a loan against the value of your insurance policy, you are borrowing your own money. This is not true. In reality, you are borrowing money from the insurance company, and using the cash value of your policy as collateral.

Some advantages of these type of loans are:

- The interest you will have to pay is usually lower than the one charged by credit cards; and,
- This kind of loans doesn't have a fixed repayment

schedule, which can give you some flexibility to make your payments.

However, there are a few important things you should keep in mind.

- If you don't make payments, interest will accrue, and if you don't pay it, the interest will be added to your loan balance increasing the amount you owe.
- In case you don't make any payments, your increased loan balance could reach an amount equal to your policy's value, and then the insurance company will terminate (also called surrender) your policy and use the cash proceeds from the surrender to pay off the loan balance. This could produce an adverse tax effect for you.

So, if you decide to take advantage of the benefits of this kind of loan while avoiding their main risks you should:

- Monitor your balance and compare it with the cash value of your policy;
- Regularly make payments on the loan;
- Pay the interest on your loan in cash.
- If for any circumstance you were unable to pay your loan, contact your insurance company and discuss with them your options.

5. Renegotiate with creditors

Let's say you have evaluated all the options analyzed before to consolidate your debts and reduce the amount of interest you would have to pay, but none of them seems viable. Maybe you don't own a home, don't have a 401(k) plan or a relative or friend you could reach out for financial help. If that's your case, and you cannot manage your current amount of debt, then it might be time to contact your creditors.

Explain to them what's your situation and why you are in it. It could be because of recent unemployment, underemployment because you lost a part-time or second job, or as a consequence of a sudden medical emergency.

Tell your creditors that even when you would like to pay down your balance with them, unless they can give you better terms you definitely won't be able to do it.

It is crucial that you don't wait too long to approach your creditors. Don't wait until you have made several monthly payments late or worse, not at all, and your account is about to be closed and turn to a collection agency.

Your creditors know it is in their best interest to try to reach an agreement with you on some terms that could allow you to repay your debt, instead of risking putting you in a position where you are forced to look for a settlement or have to file for bankruptcy.

If you think you won't be able to handle these negotiations with your creditors, or you don't wish to do it yourself, then you should approach a reputable nonprofit credit counseling organization for help. These organizations provide their services for free or at a little cost and have trained professionals working as credit counselors that can help you create a manageable budget. They can negotiate with your creditors better payment terms to develop a realistic debt management plan.

Obviously, it is essential to make sure the credit counseling service you are going to work with is legitimate. Otherwise, it will try to charge you hidden fees that very quickly can add up or propose strategies that even if in the end allow you to liquidate your debt, could affect your credit score negatively.

You can find a credit counselor by contacting the National Foundation for Credit Counseling (nfcc.org/), which is the largest nonprofit financial counseling organization in the country. Another option is the U.S. Trustee Program (justice.gov/ust/list-credit-counseling-agencies-approved-pursuant-11-usc-111), which, as part of the U.S. Department of Justice, offers information about approved credit counseling agencies by state.

6. Debt Settlement

Evidently, the responsible, honest, and right thing to do is to do your best to repay all your debts. We have already explored multiple options and strategies you could use to do just that. However, what can you do if, after a careful analysis of all available ways to repay your debts, you conclude that you have put yourself in a situation where, unfortunately, repayment may not be possible?

Then you must consider the last two possible options: debt settlement and filing for bankruptcy.

Debt settlement is the arrangement you as a debtor reach with your creditors to liquidate your debt by making one lump sum payment for an amount smaller than the total debt you owe. Creditors accept a debt settlement because it allows them to recover more money than what they could expect to receive if you declare bankruptcy.

How Does It Work?

You can negotiate a debt settlement yourself, or you can hire the services of a debt settlement company or even a lawyer (any of these two last options will cost you). In the latter cases, you will stop making payments to your creditors and instead you will send that money to the settlement company (or your attorney), which will put those funds in a savings account. When the funds reach a certain amount, the settlement company will contact your creditors and start negotiating.

Once it agrees with the lender about the sum of the settlement, it pays the creditor and takes a fee for its services. That settlement fee can be a fixed amount or a percentage of the debt that was canceled. After you settled one debt, the process starts again with another debt. If you decide to hire the services of a settlement company or a lawyer, you need to do your homework and make sure they have the right record, experience, and reputation.

A debt settlement can only work with unsecured loans, such as credit cards or personal loans, given that in the case of loans with collateral (like your house or car), the lender will follow the process to repossess the asset offered as collateral and will not agree to negotiate a different form of payment. Creditors only settle when accounts are a few months past due, so, if you are current with your payments or just one or two months behind, debt settlement might not be an option.

Advantages

What are the benefits of reaching a debt settlement with your creditors?

- As already mentioned, one of them is the fact that you could have the total balance of your debt canceled for good, by making a lump sum payment for a smaller amount than what you owe (20-30% less or maybe even more).
- The process to reach a debt settlement and its execution can take significantly less time than what it would have normally taken to pay your debt (even using debt

consolidation or credit counseling) or to follow a bankruptcy process.

- And probably the most positive aspect of debt settlement is that it could help you avoid bankruptcy.

Disadvantages

What are the disadvantages of debt settlement?

- As I mentioned before, creditors usually only settle when accounts are a few months past due. During that time the late payments are reported to the credit bureaus, and this obviously hurts your credit score. Additionally, those late payments will remain on your credit report for up to seven years, making it difficult for you to get new credit cards or loans, and maybe even affecting the insurance rates you are offered.
- Also, even if you can settle with your creditors, the information in the corresponding accounts will be updated in your credit report as "Charged-Off Settled" or "Paid-Settled," instead of the traditional "Paid in Full." Because of this, it may take a few months (maybe more), until you can be approved again for an unsecured credit.
- Another aspect that needs to be remembered is the fact that the Internal Revenue Service (IRS) considers the portion of your total debt that is forgiven by the lenders, as income that you should include on your tax return. So you need to plan accordingly.

13

BANKRUPTCY

In this chapter we will address the last option to deal with a debt problem: filing for bankruptcy. The bankruptcy system provides for an individual or business, an opportunity to have a new start by eliminating part of their debts or repay them under the protection of the bankruptcy court.

Types of Bankruptcy

There are six different types of bankruptcy, usually known by the title of the chapter of the Federal Bankruptcy Act in which they appear, but the two most common types that apply to individuals are Chapter 7 and Chapter 13 bankruptcies.

Chapter 7 Bankruptcy

In a Chapter 7 bankruptcy, you ask the court to cancel (discharge is the legal term) most of your unsecured debts, such as credit cards and medical bills. In exchange for this, a bankruptcy trustee, who is an officer of the Department of Justice, can take property you own and sell it to use the proceeds to pay your creditors in the order established by the Bankruptcy Code.

You can keep some of your assets, which cannot be used to repay your creditors. Those assets, called exempt assets, are determined by every state in its laws and typically they include:

- Some of the equity you might have in your house called the homestead exemption. The federal homestead exemption amount is currently $23,675 as of 2016 (double that if you are a married couple filing a joint bankruptcy). This amount is adjusted every three years in April, and the last adjustment occurred in 2016.
- The cash value of your insurance policies.
- Most retirement plans and benefits.
- Some personal property such as household goods, furniture, appliances, books and musical instruments.
- Jewelry worth up to $1,000 or so, and a vehicle in which your equity doesn't exceed a few thousand dollars.
- Tools you use for your job, at least up to a few thousand dollars.
- All public benefits, like welfare, social security or unemployment insurance.
- While these exemptions aren't significant, at least they avoid your having to start over with absolutely nothing.

Once all your non-exempt liquid assets have been liquidated, and the proceeds distributed to your creditors, any remaining debt is discharged. This means that neither your creditors nor any third-party collectors should try to collect that debt from you.

Some debts like alimony, child support, and certain tax debts cannot be discharged and subsist regardless of your filing for bankruptcy. Student loans are usually not dischargeable because even when they could be under certain conditions, those conditions are very tough to meet.

Chapter 13 Bankruptcy

In a Chapter 13 bankruptcy, sometimes called the "wage-earner plan," when you file for bankruptcy you submit a repayment plan that would make it possible to pay back all or part of your debts over a three to five-year period. How much you have to repay and how long can you take to do it will depend on your income, the amount and types of debt you owe, and how much do you have in assets.

The bankruptcy trustee and creditors can object to various aspects of the plan. Once you submit the payment plan, you must start making payments to the court (even if the plan has not been approved yet), who then will pay your creditors.

You basically surrender control of your finances to the bankruptcy court and a percentage of your regular income is used to pay off your creditors. While the approved repayment plan is in place, your debt doesn't generate interest charges and your creditors are not allowed to pressure you for payment.

When all the conditions of the court are finally fulfilled, you receive an official discharge which clears you of any further obligation to your creditors and emerge debt-free from the bankruptcy.

Which Bankruptcy Should You Use?

There are very detailed eligibility requirements you must satisfy to be able to file for Chapter 7 or Chapter 13 bankruptcy. If you meet the requirements for both, you can choose which one makes more sense for your situation, but in many cases, you don't have a choice.

The law tries to limit access to Chapter 7 bankruptcy just to people who truly can't pay their debts given their income. You can check if you are eligible to file for bankruptcy under Chapter 7 by using the calculator in legalconsumer.com.

Disabled veterans whose debts were incurred during active duty and people whose debts originated fundamentally from the operation of a business are exempt from having to satisfy these eligibility requirements and get a pass to file Chapter 7 bankruptcy.

You cannot file for Chapter 7 bankruptcy, among other cases, if you already did it within the last eight years and obtained a discharge of your debts, or if you did it under Chapter 13 within the previous six years.

It's important also to mention that even if you qualify and can file for bankruptcy, the court can dismiss your case if it thinks there are elements to consider that you engaged in activities to try to cheat your creditors or concealed assets you wanted to keep.

To be eligible to file for Chapter 13 bankruptcy you will need to demonstrate to the bankruptcy court that you have enough income, once you subtract certain allowed expenses and required payments on secured debts, to cover your repayment obligations.

For your payment plan to be confirmed or approved and allowed proceeding, it must contemplate paying different types of debts in a variety of ways, considering the stipulations of the Bankruptcy Code applicable to every class of creditor claim.

Other key requirements to file for Chapter 13 are:

1. You must be current on your taxes. You have to submit

proof that you filed your federal and state income tax returns for the previous four years to your bankruptcy filing date.

2. Your debts cannot exceed certain limits. Your secured debts cannot exceed $1,184,200, and your unsecured debts $394,725. These amounts are adjusted periodically to recognize the impact of inflation. Their next adjustment will be in April 2019.

Things to consider before filing for bankruptcy

Just based on what we have mentioned until now, you can appreciate that filing for bankruptcy is far from being a simple and straightforward process. Additionally, there are other factors that you need to take into consideration before deciding to file for bankruptcy.

A. Bankruptcy documents can be confusing

To file for bankruptcy, you need to prepare a series of forms (known as bankruptcy schedules and go from A through J). These forms can be rather complicated and not particularly easy to understand in some cases. Because of this circumstance, having the advice of an experienced bankruptcy attorney can be helpful to avoid making any mistakes that could have an adverse impact on your property, finances, or even put at risk your freedom.

B. Your financial affairs will become public

Someone filing for bankruptcy will have not only to provide a lot of information about his or her financial transactions but also attend a public meeting called "meeting of creditors," and answer a series of questions to the trustee about the information contained in the filing. Any of the creditors of the debtor (and their attorneys) may attend and also ask questions about your financial affairs.

C. The Bankruptcy process can take a while

You should not expect the bankruptcy process to be concluded fast. The process for a Chapter 7 bankruptcy usually takes between four and six months, and for a Chapter 13 from three to five years.

D. Filing for bankruptcy can be expensive

It can surprise many people to know, that filing for bankruptcy can have a significant cost, especially for someone who already is in a precarious financial situation. Obviously, the cost will vary depending on whether an attorney is hired, but it can cost from a few hundred to thousands of dollars.
If you retain the services of a bankruptcy attorney, the cost can vary a lot, depending on what state you live, the characteristics of the attorney, and the complexity of your bankruptcy case. However, many attorneys offer free consultations to discuss whether you really need to file for bankruptcy, what would your options be, and to estimate what could be your total cost, so it might be a good idea to talk with a few of them.

E. Absolute honesty is required during the process

You must sign your bankruptcy papers under "penalty of perjury" swearing that everything in them is true. The position of the bankruptcy courts is that only an honest debtor is entitled to a discharge of debt. Conducts such as the failure to disclose debts or assets, or providing false information under oath might be considered to constitute bankruptcy fraud, which is a federal crime.

Any creditor of a bankruptcy debtor can also file a complaint seeking to deny the debtor a discharge for bankruptcy fraud, establishing the debt owed by the creditor should be not dischargeable because the credit was obtained fraudulently.

F. Loss of Property

Very probably you will lose any property you cannot successfully convince the court that should be considered part of the "exempt property" that the law explicitly allows you to keep (under Chapter 7).

G. The Discharge is Personal

We already discussed how a bankruptcy discharge releases a debtor from liability for certain debts, which means the debtor no longer is required to pay those debts that are discharged. However, it is essential to understand that the effect of the discharge is personal, it only protects the debtor who filed for bankruptcy, and doesn't eliminate the debt itself. In the case of debts where there are co-signers (like for example on a home or school loan), the lender can seek to collect the debt from the other co-signer or co-signers of the loan.

Take this into consideration if you have as co-signers any family members or friends who won't file for bankruptcy.

H. The Effect of Bankruptcy on Your Credit

Legally, a Chapter 7 bankruptcy stays on an individual's credit report for ten years from the date of filing the petition.
A Chapter 13 bankruptcy remains on an individual's credit report for seven years.
In practice, to return to the fair score someone had before he or she filed for bankruptcy (650-699 range), it could take around five years, assuming that person starts following better credit practices.

PART III

STEPS YOU NEED TO TAKE TO CONTROL YOUR MONEY

14

TAKE CONTROL OF YOUR FINANCES

Now, you should put into practice what you have learned in the previous chapters to take control of your finances and increase your net worth. To do that, you need to take four key steps.

Step 1 - Identify Your Current Financial Situation. Calculate Your Net Worth

First, to determine whether any effort you put into improving your finances is working and producing the results you expect or not, you have to identify what is the current situation of your finances. The way to do that is to calculate your net worth.

As mentioned before (Chapter 3), your net worth primarily represents where you are financially at some point in time, like today or at the end of last month or last week. It tells you how much money you have or, if your net worth is negative, how much money you owe.

To calculate your net worth, you make a list that includes all your assets, and another including all your debts. Once you have those lists, you subtract from your total assets the amount corresponding to your total debts and that gives you your net worth.

While calculating your net worth once is helpful, the real value comes from figuring it on a regular basis (at least every six months or every year.) Doing so will allow you not only to see how your net worth changes over time, but much more important, to evaluate whether your finances are improving, and identify those areas that require more attention. Keep this in mind when choosing which tool you will use to calculate and store your net worth information.

Step 2 - Make a Budget

A budget is a fundamental planning tool that helps you to keep your finances in order, by allowing you to prioritize and control your expenses and your savings, while also keeping track of your spending patterns.

The idea behind a budget is straightforward. Once you have estimated all your income and expenses, subtract the expenses from your income. If you have a surplus, you can then determine what to do with that money, save it, invest it or spend it. If your expenses are higher than your income, then you will have to adjust your budget by looking for those expenses you could reduce or even eliminate or look for ways to increase your income.

Any method to create a personal budget involves making projections about your income and expenditures. The income and expense categories that need to be included in the budget will depend on your situation. Among the most common income categories to include are:

- Salary or professional fees
- Bonuses
- Interest and dividends
- Rents and royalties
- Retirement income (pension, social security, retirement account withdrawals)
- Alimony
- Child support
- Tips

Common expense categories (and subcategories) include:

- Housing (mortgage or rent, home or renters insurance, HOA -homeowners association fees-, etc.)
- Food (groceries and dining out)
- Healthcare (insurance premiums, deductibles, copays, doctors, dentist, medicines, lab tests, etc.)
- Personal (clothing, personal care -hair, nails-, gym, etc.)
- Insurance (liability and life)
- Transportation: (cars -loan or lease, insurance, gas, maintenance-; train, subway, taxis, Uber, Lyft, tolls, etc.)
- Utilities (phone, Internet, electricity, gas, cable, water, etc.)
- Entertainment (Books, movies, sports, concerts, hobbies, etc.)
- Savings (Emergency fund, retirement, specific goals (car, trip, wedding, etc.))
- Gifts
- Donations
- Education (Books, courses, tuition, supplies, etc.)
- Taxes (federal, state and local).

If you have not been keeping records of all this information, you can start by using your payroll or invoices for professional fees, and your bank, credit card, and department stores statements (if you have any store card).

Gather all that info and put it in a spreadsheet, or if you prefer, you can use a personal finance management application. Practically all personal finance applications allow you to create a budget. Some of them will even help you by suggesting categories for your income and expenses, based on the information contained in your bank and credit card statements, when you electronically download that info into the applications.

You can use as a starting point that you can adjust later, the average amount you have been earning or spending in those same categories in the past.

There are two main benefits of creating a budget. First, you will be able to keep your spending in line with your income to avoid generating debt. Secondly, you can prioritize those things that have a positive impact on the health of your finances, such as paying your bills on time, pay down and manage your debt, build a safety net, and save for short, medium, and long-term goals.

Let's analyze now in a little more detail, a few things that you should do to maximize those two main benefits.

Control Lifestyle Inflation

The phenomenon usually known as lifestyle inflation refers to the situation in which, as people advance in their professional careers and their income increases, their level of spending also tends to increase, generally in the same proportion or, in some cases, unfortunately even at a higher level.

Many people fall into the trap of conspicuous consumption, trying to get some level of social validation or recognition of their professional success.

This situation tends to have a very adverse effect in the long term, because it limits the ability of people to save, invest, and in general to build wealth, reducing as a consequence the funds available to them during their retirement.

Many studies have shown that a considerable percentage of people with above-average incomes have a somewhat precarious financial situation, mostly because of excessive spending. Don't fall into that trap. If you tend to adjust your expectations and your spending in response to an increase in your income, the additional revenue won't feel like such for long, and you will burn it all.

An excellent strategy to avoid this from happening is to save automatically and invest at least half of any increase in income you have. By doing this, you contribute to your long-term saving goals, without feeling that you must restrict your spending.

Recognize the Difference Between Needs and Wants

This is a tough one for many people, and particularly in our current society where a lot of people seem to feel entitled to almost anything.

Being able to establish the difference between needs and wants rationally and acting in consequence, can have a dramatic effect not only in your spending level but also in your level of satisfaction and happiness with your standard of living.

In most cases, it should be easy to differentiate between a need and a want. A need is something we require to survive (food, shelter, essential clothing, health and personal care, transportation, and communication for example), while what you want is something that it would just be nice to have. So, we need a car, but we might want a luxury or a sports car. We need clothing, but we might want clothes of a particular brand or from a specific designer.

The difference is clear, but the problem is that too many times we look for ways to rationalize unneeded and even extravagant purchases, trying to justify them under the guise of covering a need. When we do that, the difference in cost between what we could have bought to satisfy a real need, and what we bought because we wanted it, represents the amount of our unnecessary spending.

Always try to spend mindfully and don't shop as entertainment or as some therapy.

Look for Opportunities to Reduce or Eliminate Expenses

It is essential always to keep an eye on your expenses. Periodically review them (at least every six months), comparing them to your budget, and to your expenses during the previous year.

You can do this very quickly by just generating a report, using any of the multiple available personal finance desktop or online applications. You will probably find that some expenses have increased without you noticing, and this exercise will give you an opportunity to look for avoidable expenses or for those that you could at least reduce.

Look for example for all those expenses that correspond to subscriptions for services you are no longer using, or not often enough to justify keeping the subscription. It could be subscriptions to magazines, newspapers, cable channels, a club or gym, an online service, etc.

Identify which are your more important expenses every month and evaluate if there is any way to reduce them. Maybe there are new cable, internet, or cellular phone plans available that would represent some monthly savings while keeping the same or even better levels of service.

Finally, don't forget to look for those small expenses that you end up having to pay with some frequency, such as bank fees for using ATMs, not keeping a minimum balance or something similar, and look for ways to eliminate them.

Be realistic when deciding which expenses to eliminate. You should aim to reach a reasonable level of frugality that you can sustain over the long-term.

Pay Down and Manage Existing and New Debt

With the help of a budget—and a cash flow report—instead of merely guessing, you can schedule all the necessary payments to make sure you can liquidate your current debts. Additionally, if you see the need to use credit to buy something, you can evaluate in detail how much credit you could handle with your current level of income and expenses, and how long it would take you to pay it down. All this, without affecting your capacity to cover your existing obligations, as well as your saving goals.

Build a Safety Net

One of the best things you can do to protect your finances is to be prepared and take steps to minimize the negative impact that some situations, such as a disease, accident, or unemployment among others, can have on your finances.

There are usually two ways to deal with those eventualities.

The first is to create an emergency fund of at least the equivalent of six months' worth of living expenses (more if possible).

It is best to keep this money in an account separate from your checking account. Doing that makes it easy to manage the fund and also reduces the temptation of using the money you save there for other purposes. In some cases, it might even be a good idea to open that account with a different bank, making it a little harder to make transfers between accounts.

Put saving for this fund as a regular expense item in your budget. Keep in mind that having an emergency fund is an ongoing effort. It is probable that as soon as you fund it, you might need to use it, and in that case, you will have to start the process of building the fund again.

The second way to manage some of those eventualities is to buy insurance that would limit the financial impact of that kind of situations. For example, disability insurance can cover a significant portion of your income if you were suddenly unable to work, and health insurance will reduce the cost of medical treatment you or your family might need.

The main idea behind buying any insurance is that, by making a rather small effort now, you can avoid having your finances derailed in the future, if or when one of the risks covered by your insurance policies becomes a reality.

Establish Saving Goals and Automate Them

Start saving for all those goals you have, like buying a new car or house, taking a long vacation, pay for your kid's college, or your retirement.

First, run your numbers and determine precisely how much you can save. Then, to make it easy to follow through with your saving efforts, set up an automatic transfer to move those funds from the checking account where you deposit your paycheck or any other primary source of income, to your savings account,

401(k), or IRA account. This way you won't give yourself the opportunity to have second thoughts about saving that money.

Most financial advisors recommend that you save around 15% of your income for your retirement, preferably in a 401(k) account if you have access to one at work, and particularly when your employer offers to match or contribute a percentage of what you save. If you don't have access to a 401(k), then open an individual retirement account (IRA or Roth IRA).

It is crucial that you start saving for your retirement as early as possible so that you take full advantage of the powerful effect of compounding, which mainly refers to the reinvestment of any interests, dividends or capital gains that your savings and investments produce. The longer you can reinvest those earnings, the higher the final value of your investments will be.

Take Advantage of the Power of Compound Growth

Compound growth is commonly defined as the rate at which an investment grows over a period of years (or a company or a country's economy). However, the most important thing to grasp of this concept, is its incredible power to generate wealth over time, when you invest in financial assets that produce interests, dividends, or capital gains and you reinvest them into the original investment.

Let's review some examples that will show very clearly the unbelievable power of compound growth.

	Person 1		Person 2	
Years	Amount Saved Per Year	Savings Accumulated	Amount Saved Per Year	Savings Accumulated
1	$ 6,000	$ 6,300		
2	$ 6,000	$ 12,915		
3	$ 6,000	$ 19,861		
4	$ 6,000	$ 27,154		
5	$ 6,000	$ 34,811		
6	$ 6,000	$ 42,852		
7	$ 6,000	$ 51,295		
8	$ 6,000	$ 60,159		
9	$ 6,000	$ 69,467		
10	$ 6,000	$ 79,241		
11		$ 83,203	$ 6,000	$ 6,300
12		$ 87,363	$ 6,000	$ 12,915
13		$ 91,731	$ 6,000	$ 19,861
14		$ 96,318	$ 6,000	$ 27,154
15		$ 101,133	$ 6,000	$ 34,811
16		$ 106,190	$ 6,000	$ 42,852
17		$ 111,500	$ 6,000	$ 51,295
18		$ 117,075	$ 6,000	$ 60,159
19		$ 122,928	$ 6,000	$ 69,467
20		$ 129,075	$ 6,000	$ 79,241
21		$ 135,529	$ 6,000	$ 89,503
22		$ 142,305	$ 6,000	$ 100,278
23		$ 149,420	$ 6,000	$ 111,592
24		$ 156,891	$ 6,000	$ 123,471
25		**$ 164,736**	$ 6,000	**$ 135,945**

In the chart above, you can see the different results two persons could have depending on their savings during 25 years. The example supposes that both persons saved $6,000 per year, and they gained 5% annually. We will assume that they saved that amount at the beginning of the year to simplify the calculations.

Person 1 started saving from year one, continued to do it for ten years and then stopped. At the end of twenty-five years finished with $164,736.

Person 2 didn't begin saving until year eleven but continued doing it for the next fifteen years. Despite having saved $30,000 and five years more than Person 1, Person 2 ended up with only $135,945, which is 17% less.

After looking at an example like this, it becomes evident the amazing effect that the accumulation of reinvested returns can have on the growth of some financial assets, and how important it is to begin saving and investing as early as possible to generate future wealth.

By the way, if in the previous example another person had saved the same $6,000 per year but during every one of the 25 years, that person would finish with $300,681. That is precisely why you should start saving for your retirement as soon as you can, so that you can take full advantage of the powerful effect of compounding.

Unfortunately, the importance of the concept of compounding to grow wealth is not emphasized as much as it should, and therefore, its power is not entirely understood or appreciated by most people, especially the young, who for obvious reasons are the ones who can take better advantage of it.

I would have loved it, if some teacher had shown me examples like these, to help me grasp the importance of compound growth when I was in high school or at least during college.

Step 3 - Monitor your Cash Flow

The third and very important step you need to take is to monitor your cash flow.

As we discussed in Chapter 2, having a perfectly crafted budget won't necessarily guarantee you will have the liquidity required to cover all your financial obligations on time. You can only be sure of that, once you run your cash flow considering the exact dates on which you expect to receive income or pay for expenses, and see you will stay cash flow positive during the whole period you are evaluating. Otherwise, you will need to reschedule some expense or expenses to a different date that would give you the necessary liquidity to cover on time all your obligations.

Remember, never rely just on a budget, because if you do, sooner or later you may find yourself not having the funds required to cover some payment.

Step 4 - Pay Your Bills on Time

It would be hard to overstate the importance of having access to credit, and your credit score can determine whether you get credit, and how much you have to pay for it. Lenders use your credit score to try to predict how likely it is that you will repay a loan and make payments on time.

In the next chapter, we will talk in more detail about what is your credit score and how it works. For the moment suffice it to say that to determine it, five groups of elements are taken into consideration, and of those, the one that has most weight is the one represented by your payment history. After all, lenders' primary interest is not only to find out if you pay your bills but also how promptly. This is why making sure you schedule and pay your bills on time is so important.

There are multiple applications for your computer, mobile device or phone, that can help you not only schedule and keep track of your income and expenses but also give you the option to set up reminders, so you don't forget to make any payments you owe on a timely manner.

15

YOUR CREDIT SCORE

It is difficult to overestimate the impact that your credit score can have on your finances.

As I mentioned before, it will influence not only your ability to access credit and how much you will pay for it, but also your opportunities to be considered for some jobs, and even the cost of the premiums you will pay for insurance. Because of this, you should know what it is, and understand how it works.

It All Begins with Your Credit Report

Your credit score is calculated based on what is reflected in your credit report. All the information about how you pay your bills, repay your loans, what debts you have, and how much credit you have available, as well as some additional data that will help any potential lender determine if you represent a low or high credit risk is accumulated in your credit report. As a result, every time there are significant changes in your credit report, your credit score will also change.

All this information is collected by the credit reporting agencies (CRAs, also known as credit bureaus), who receive it from merchants, lenders, landlords, etc. The information included in your credit report includes several sections:

• **Personal Information.** Such as your name, address (current and previous), social security number, phone number, birth date, and employers (present and past).

• **Credit History.** In here is your paying history for all kind of companies that provided you with credit: banks, retail stores, finance and mortgage institutions, etc. There is information about when the account was opened, type of account, the amount of credit granted or amount loaned, your monthly payments, if you are current with your payments, if those payments have been on time, if you have missed any of them, etc.

• **Public Records.** This section contains information that is available in public records that could help lenders decide your level of creditworthiness like court judgments, bankruptcies, or tax liens.

• **Report Inquiries.** Here is the information about all the companies or institutions who have requested a copy of your credit report. Also a list of enterprises who have received just limited info about you (like your name and address), when you meet certain criteria that identify you as part of a target group to whom they want to offer some credit or products. These are the companies that send you "pre-approved" credit card and lines of credit offers.

• **Disputed Statements.** If you have made any statements disputing information contained in your report, they will be here, together with any related statements made by your creditors.

While your credit report includes all this information, it doesn't say how risky you could be as a debtor. The lenders have to make that decision themselves based on the data, and as you can imagine, analyzing all that data can be complicated and take some time.

To address that need, in the late 50s, a company called Fair, Issac and Company (currently FICO) began working to develop a credit scoring system that could integrate all the information contained in the credit report and synthesize it in a simple number. At the end of the 80s, they launched what is known as its general-purpose FICO score.

The "base" FICO score which is broadly used, falls within a range that goes from 300 to 850 points, divided into five different levels: poor, fair, good, very good, and excellent (other industry-specific scores range from 250 to 900 points.)

FICO Credit Score Range		
Score	**Range**	**Population**
Excellent	800+	20%
Very Good	740-799	16.60%
Good	670-739	13%
Fair	580-669	19.90%
Poor	579 or less	10.30%

Factors That Determine Your Credit Score

While the exact algorithm used to determine the score is proprietary information owned by FICO, an accepted breakdown of the main factors affecting its determination is:

- 35% of the score is based on everything related to your payment history.
- 30% on your level of outstanding debt in relation to your available credit and your annual income. Not only your

total credit utilization ratio is important (what percentage of your total cumulative credit available you have used and owe), but also the credit utilization ratio of every individual credit account. It is usually recommended that you keep your balances at 25% or less of every credit limit you have available. The only exception to this recommendation would be when you are following a credit consolidation strategy (as mentioned earlier), to make your debts more manageable and easy to pay.
- 15% is based on the length of time during which you have had credit. The longer, the better, because this gives lenders more information to predict your future behavior as a debtor.
- 10% on the existence of new credit.
- 10% on the variety of types of credit you have. It helps to have different kinds of credit accounts, like for example credit cards (revolving credit) and a car loan or mortgage (installment loan.)

Factors that can have an adverse (short-term) effect on your score are:

- Opening new credit accounts; and,
- If several lenders (authorized by you) inquire about your credit, during the previous year (these are known as hard inquiries).

When the inquiries are made during a short period, probably because of your shopping around for the best offer for a particular credit, they don't affect your score. Neither when potential lenders look at your credit score for marketing purposes (also known as soft inquiries.) But too many "hard inquiries" over a period, negatively affects your score since potential lenders will think you may be getting into additional debt.

It's important to mention that the three major CRAs (Equifax, Experian, and TransUnion) have their own scoring systems, which are based on the one originally developed by FICO.

How to Improve Your Credit Score

There are some things you can do to try to improve your credit score.

- Periodically review your credit report and fix any errors. Do it every quarter or six months. Once a year at least.
- Because of the importance of the credit utilization ratio we already mentioned, try to keep old credit accounts open even when you are no longer using them often. Obviously, this makes it a good practice when evaluating credit cards, to give preference to those that don't charge an annual fee.
- Reduce the balance on your credit cards as much as possible. As noted before, keeping your balance at 25% or less of your authorized credit limit would be ideal.
- Pay your bills on time. This is the best way to see a steady improvement on your credit score.
- Carefully shop for a loan. Make sure that all inquiries to your credit report by the lenders you are considering take place within a few weeks. This way they will be counted as only one inquiry of your credit score.
- Don't open new credit accounts too close to the date when you are planning to apply for a large loan (like a mortgage.) It would have an adverse impact on your score.

You have some rights regarding your credit information, based on the Fair Credit Reporting Act (FCRA) enacted by the Federal Trade Commission in 1971 to regulate the credit reporting companies. The FCRA:

- Guarantees your access to your credit report.
- It establishes that when someone denies you credit (or even employment) because of something in your credit report, that person or organization must tell you why, and you can contact the credit bureau who provided that information.
- Gives you the right to dispute any mistake or inaccurate information included in your credit report, and provides the corresponding CRA 30 days to review it. If you can prove the mistake or inaccuracy, then that data must be removed or corrected within 30 days. The disputed information, until proven accurate, cannot be included in your credit report without the CRA including a copy of your written dispute along with it.
- Gives you the right to request that your name is removed from the lists the CRAs sell to marketers.

SUMMARY

Part I. The Basic Framework

You need a basic framework to understand and take control of your finances. That framework is composed of three central concepts.

1. Money Quadrants
2. Cash Flow
3. Net Worth

The Money Quadrants (Chapter 1)

Every financial transaction you do falls into one of the money quadrants: Income, Expenses, Assets, and Debt.

Income Quadrant (Chapter 2)

It covers all types of income you can receive, which can be classified into three main groups:

- **Active Income.** It depends directly on your efforts (i.e., salary or professional fees).
- **Passive Income.** It's generated by different kinds of assets you might own and independently of any direct effort on your part, such as financial assets, personal, real estate or intellectual property or equity in a business.
- **Aleatory Income.** It's unexpected (winning the lottery, receiving a legacy, etc.)

Expenses Quadrant (Chapter 3)

It covers any type of expenses you can have, which are classified into four groups:

- **Primary Expenses.** Correspond to any expenses related to basic living needs (food, housing, healthcare, etc.)
- **Secondary Expenses.** Those related to improvements in your quality of life once your basic needs have been satisfied.
- **Debt Service.** Any expenses that correspond to the payment of any kind of debt.
- **Aleatory Expenses.** Originated by unexpected events or circumstances (accidents, disease, etc.)
- **Savings.** Not strictly an expense, but savings need to be considered here because they should be a category in your budget.

Assets Quadrant (Chapter 4)

It includes any type of assets you can have, which are classified into five groups:

- **Financial Investments.** Any kind: certificates of deposit

(CDs), savings accounts, mutual funds, ETFs (electronic exchanged funds), bonds, options, futures, etc.

- **Personal Property.** Such as vehicles, jewelry, antiques, collectibles, etc.
- **Real Estate Property.** Your home and any kind of rental property.
- **Business Equity.** When you have any participation in the ownership of a business.
- **Intellectual Property.** Created or owned by you and that generates royalties.

Debt Quadrant (Chapter 5)

It covers any type of debt you can have: secured or unsecured, with a fixed or variable rate, a fixed or variable payment term, revolving, mortgages, installment debt, etc.

Cash Flow (Chapters 6-7)

The concept of cash flow is based on the relation that exists between the income and expenses quadrants. To analyze your cash flow, you determine what will be the balance between your expected income and expenses during a specific period (a month or a quarter for example).

That cash flow balance can be positive (your income is higher than your expenses), balanced (your income and expenses are equal), or negative (when your expenses are higher than your income).

Because not having the necessary funds to make a payment to which you are contractually obligated could have a negative effect on your finances, constantly monitoring your cash flow is essential.

Net Worth (Chapter 8)

The concept of net worth is based on the relation that exists between the assets and debt quadrants.

You calculate your net worth by subtracting from the total value of your assets on a date (at the end of a month, quarter or year), the total amount of your debts. The result will tell you how much you are worth financially or how much you owe.

Monitoring your net worth periodically (every quarter, semester or year), allows you to determine if your finances are in order, and how well have you used and managed all the income you have had until that point.

It is fundamental that you increase your net worth, at least to a level where you will have enough money to pay for all your expenses during retirement.

Don't confuse having a high income with having a high net worth. Many people with high incomes have a low net worth. Studies show that having the right spending and saving habits is much more important to reach a high net worth.

Two cycles can have a significant but a very different impact on your net worth.

The **Active Income Replacement Cycle (AIRC)** will help you increase your net worth. The AIRC forms when you have a positive cash flow and invest your income that exceeds your expenses in an asset which generates passive income. Then that passive income contributes to your having a positive cash flow again, and the cycle repeats. The effect of the AIRC is that your passive income grows as a percentage of your total income, at the same time your net worth also increases.

On the other hand, the **Deb Creation Cycle (DCC)** is formed when your expenses exceed your income, forcing you to use your net worth or incur on new debt to cover the deficit, until your net worth is depleted and/or your debt reaches an unmanageable level.

Part II. Understanding Debt

Understanding Debt (Chapter 9)

In its purest form, debt is a way or means to make it possible to buy things we cannot afford.

The most important conditions on debt are the term for repayment and the amount of interest rate.

About the repayment type, debt can have a fixed payment term (it is set to be paid off by a specific date, like a mortgage), or a variable repayment method (as in the case of credit cards or lines of credit).

Concerning the interest rates, there are two basic types: fixed and variable. When the interest rate is variable, lenders charge some points over a benchmark rate, so the rate the borrower has to pay is set as "prime rate (or any other benchmark rate) + X%." Multiple factors will influence the interest rate you have to pay: your record as a debtor, inflation expectations, the length of time the money will be lent out, the liquidity of the debt (how easy would be for the lender to sell his or her rights to the loan), etc.

Why So Many People Overspend? (Chapter 10)

In general, debt is only considered good, when it helps you increase your net worth by allowing you to buy an asset that will increase its value or make it possible for you to generate long-term income. Examples of good debt are:

- A mortgage (for a house with the right price, location, and condition);
- A student loan (for the right amount considering the earnings you could generate later);
- The debt you have to incur to cover unexpected events (like sickness or an accident) not covered by your insurance.

The use of credit cards is only advisable when the cards offer you benefits (points or cash back) that exceed their annual cost, and you liquidate the full balance every month.

Many people (more than a third) spend more money than what they earn. The two leading causes are lack of financial knowledge and personal discipline.

How Much Debt is Too Much? (Chapter 11)

At the end of the second quarter of 2018 total consumer debt was more than $13 trillion. The main kinds of debt were mortgages, student loans, car loans, and credit cards.

The average U.S. household owed $134,058 and was using on average 9.8% of their disposable income (income left after taxes have been paid) on debt service.

To evaluate your debt load, you should calculate your debt-to-income ratio. You should do it in two ways.

In the first one just divide your total monthly debt payments by your monthly income and multiply the result by 100. Your debt-to-income ratio here should be under 36%; 30% or under is considered excellent, and 40% or more means you are in trouble.

The second way measures only your bad debt or what is called debt overload. Here the process is the same, but instead of dividing your total monthly debts, just divide what you pay every month for credit cards and personal loans. A bad debt ratio higher than 10% is considered too high and indicates that you are overloaded with debt.

Some rules of thumb to keep your debt at manageable levels are:

- Limit housing costs to 25% or less of your net income;
- Keep your monthly car payments between 5 and 10% of your net income;
- Do not borrow to pay for a degree more than what you can realistically expect to make during your first year out of school.

How to Take Control of Your Debt (Chapter 12)

Two steps that can help you to keep your debt under control are:

- Use cash to pay for everything except your rent (or mortgage) and your car.
- Make a budget and follow it.

If your debt is already too high, two methods can be used to reduce it: the snowball and the ladder methods.

- In the snowball method, you first use all the money you have available to pay your debts (in addition to the minimum payment you are required to do) to pay your smallest debt. Once you liquidate that one, you start now paying what was the second smallest, then the third, etc. Each debt you repay will motivate you to keep going until you finally are debt free.

- In the ladder method, you start paying your most expensive debt, the one for which you are paying the highest interest rate. Once you finish you follow with the next one down and go on. This is the method that saves you more money.

To increase the benefit of the ladder method you can also use debt consolidation, which simply means to consolidate two or more debts into one that has a lower interest rate.

There are several ways to consolidate your debts:

- Transfer your balances to a credit card with a low-interest rate or no interest for a specified period;
- Use an equity loan;
- Borrow from a friend or family member;
- Borrow from your own 401(k) plan; or
- Borrow against life insurance.

If the previous options are not viable or don't work, then you could try to renegotiate with your creditors. Don't wait too long to do it. If you don't feel up to the task, approach a reputable nonprofit credit counseling organization for help.

If after exploring all the previous alternatives you realize that it will be impossible for you to pay your debt, then you should consider the possibility of reaching a settlement.

Debt settlement is the arrangement you reach with your creditors to liquidate your debt by making one lump sum payment for an amount smaller than the total debt you owe. You can handle the settlement negotiations yourself or hire a settlement company or a lawyer to do it. Any part of your debt forgiven by your debtors will be considered as income by the IRS over which you will have to pay taxes.

Bankruptcy (Chapter 13)

The two most common types of bankruptcy, from the six in the Bankruptcy Law that apply to individuals, are Chapter 7 and Chapter 13 bankruptcies.

In a Chapter 7 bankruptcy, some of your property is sold by a bankruptcy trustee, and the proceeds used to pay your debtors as much as possible of most of your unsecured debts. After that, those debts are considered canceled (discharged). Some debts like alimony, child support, and certain tax debts cannot be discharged.

In a Chapter 13 bankruptcy, you must pay back all or part of your debts over a three to five-year period, based on a repayment plan proposed by you and approved by the court. How much you have to repay and how long can you take to do it will depend on your income, the amount and types of debt you owe, and how much do you have in assets.

Before you decide to file for bankruptcy, you need to consider:

- The process and the bankruptcy documents can be confusing;
- Your financial affairs will become public;
- The process is not fast;
- Filing for bankruptcy will cost from a few hundred to thousands of dollars;
- You must be completely honest during the whole process, or you could commit a federal crime;
- Very probably you will lose some property;
- The discharge of debt is personal; and,
- It will stay on your credit report from 10 (Chapter 7) to 7 years (Chapter 13).

Part III – Steps You Need to Take to Master Your Money

Control Your Finances and Increase your Net Worth (Chapter 14)

The first step to take control of your finances is to determine your current situation. To do this, you have to calculate your net worth periodically, prepare and follow a budget to control your expenses and savings, and track your spending patterns. Also, you should constantly monitor your cash flow, to make sure you always have the necessary liquidity to cover all your financial obligations on time.

With the help of those tools you should be able to focus your efforts on:

1. Reducing and controlling your expenses. Avoid increasing your expenses every time your income increases. Recognize that just because you want something that does not mean you need it. Always look for opportunities to reduce or eliminate expenses.
2. Pay your bills on time.
3. Pay down and manage your existing and new debt.
4. Build a safety net that will allow you to handle unexpected expenses.
5. Once you have set your saving goals, look for ways to automate them by using automatic deposits or transfers.
6. Finally, start saving as soon as possible to take full advantage of the amazing results of compound growth (the cumulative effect of saving and reinvesting interests and dividends through the years).

Your Credit Score (Chapter 15)

Your credit score is calculated based on what is reflected on your credit report. The report contains all the information about how you pay your bills and repay your loans, what debts you have, and how much credit you have available. All that information is accumulated, together with some additional data that might help any potential lender determine if you represent a low or high credit risk.

The information is collected by the credit reporting agencies (CRAs, also known as credit bureaus). The three major CRAs are Equifax, Experian, and TransUnion.

The most popular scoring system is called FICO and integrates all the information contained your credit report and synthesizes it in a simple number.

The FICO score goes from 300 to 850 points divided into five levels: Poor (579 points or fewer), Fair (580 to 669), Good (670 to 739), Very Good (740 to 799), and Excellent (800 or more points).

The exact algorithm used to calculate the FICO score is proprietary info owned by the company who created it (also called FICO), but in general, it is recognized that the main factors considered, and the percentages in which they influence the score are:

- 35% based on everything related to your payment history.
- 30% on your level of outstanding debt in relation to your available credit and your annual income.
- 15% based on the length of time during which you have had credit.
- 10% based on the existence of new credit.
- 10% based on the variety of types of credit you have.

THANK YOU

Thanks for reading this book. I hope you found it useful and enjoyed reading it.

I would appreciate if you could please leave a review on Amazon. Even a line or two would be a huge help. Thank you very much.

This book is the first and an introduction to the series "Take Control of Your Finances."

ABOUT THE AUTHOR

H. Dominguez (HD) has been a business consultant for more than twenty years, working with a broad range of businesses and organizations in multiple industries. Before starting his consulting practice, he worked as a corporate lawyer in the petrochemical industry. He has always been keenly interested in personal finance and keeps the blog Money Considerations. HD lives in Connecticut.

Also by H. Dominguez:

How to Prepare for Retirement: A Simple Guide to Enjoy a Successful Retirement.

You can get in contact with HD:

Website: moneyconsiderations.com

Email: hd@moneyconsiderations.com

facebook.com/MoneyConsiderations

twitter.com/HDominguezMC

APPENDIX A - BRIEF HISTORY OF CREDIT AND DEBT

The Remote Origins

Ancient History

People have been using credit since ancient times. The concept of interest is usually attributed to the Sumerians, who lived in the region known as Mesopotamia around 4000 AD, and it seems to have derived from herding. In Sumerian, the same word was used for interest and calves. When someone lent you a herd of cattle for one year, for example, you were expected to repay by returning not only the original herd but also the calves it had produced. This growth of an asset, like cattle, was then transferred to all other commodities as well. So, while in the beginning for someone to ask for more than what had initially been lent was not considered appropriate, soon people discovered the value of "money" in relation to time.

The set of regulations and laws known as the Code of Hammurabi, enacted by the King of the same name who ruled Babylonia from 1792 to 1750 AD, already contained rules about interest, debt forgiveness, and the extension of credit. It has also been found that the Egyptians used installment sales of real estate during the time of the Pharaohs. Phoenicians, Greeks, and Romans also used credit during their extended trading along the Mediterranean.

Postclassical Era

During the period known as the Middle Ages (generally understood as covering from around the year 500 to 1500 AD), credit through the use of credit bills played an essential role in the trading activities of the many city-states common during that time, particularly in the territories of what we now know as Italy. The activities of lending and borrowing as well as buying and selling on credit were widespread practices among almost all the population; peasants, nobles, and even religious dignitaries as the Pope were involved in the use of credit and debt.

Modern History

During the period known as the Renaissance, the increase in maritime voyages contributed to the use of different forms of credit to finance those expeditions. After that, the discovery of America created new opportunities for the expansion of credit. The establishment of the first colonies in New England during the early 1600s coincides with the first recorded use of open credit at the beginning of America.

Credit and Debt in Early America

From the early days of our nation, credit has been a fundamental part of the American way of doing business. From the time when this was primarily an agrarian society, to the time when industrialization started producing the so-called "company towns," the charge accounts were typically the most common form of credit.

A charge account opened with a retailer, was also known as a store or book credit because as its name suggests, the records were kept in a ledger or book. Consumers and retailers both relied on this form of credit that didn't have the structured repayment of an installment purchase but depended on the relationship between the retailer and the consumer. Given this, the repayment schedules tended to vary based on when the consumer would have funds available. So, it was not uncommon that payments were linked more to when the crops were harvested and sold, or when factory workers received their pay.

Given the local and more personal nature of this kind of credit, one advantage was that, when consumers fell in hard times, it was not unusual for retailers to continue to extend credit to longtime, trustworthy customers, despite their limited ability to make payments for some time.

However, like it is the case also today, there were also problems given the always present risk when someone extends credit. Like today, the court system sometimes had to be involved to resolve cases of an unpaid debt.

A significant difference is that back then, and until the 1800s, people who didn't pay their debts were sent to the debtor's prison. Indeed, people unable to pay a court-ordered judgment were sentenced to these prisons, until they liquidated their debt through work or by somehow securing funds to pay the balance.

Later, with the development of more advanced bankruptcy laws, the imprisonment of people for most civil debts was restricted or eliminated.

Installment loans were also one of the earliest forms of consumer credit, and one that experienced enormous popularity and growth during the second half of the nineteenth century.

Things began to be bought using installment payments, many of which were being introduced to most American households for the first time, like cars, home appliances (sewing machines, washing machines, gas stoves, electric refrigerators, vacuum cleaners, etc.), household furniture, clothing, and farm equipment among others.

The Invention of Credit Cards

By the mid-twentieth century credit cards made their appearance. Their antecedent were some proprietary cards issued by oil companies and department stores, which were used more to try to create customer loyalty and improve customer service. These cards were accepted only by the business that issued them and in limited locations.

The original idea for the first credit card is attributed to John C. Biggins, a banker working for the Flatbush National Bank in Brooklyn, NY. It started as an experiment, as a new concept to provide credit to the community within the surrounding area of the bank.

Its clients received a card they could use to pay at stores and business in the area, and then the bank would pay the stores and assume the responsibility for collecting the debts from its customers using the card, which by the way was called "Charg-It."

This was an important innovation, because now instead of the direct relationship of the merchants providing credit to their customers, it was the bank who was paying the merchants and lending the money to its own customers.

In 1951, the Franklin National Bank located in Long Island, NY, introduced the first revolving charge card, combining the store or book credit for irregular payments, and the installment payment loans.

This innovation was well received because by using a card with revolving credit, customers could borrow money, repay it and borrow it again, without their having to be approved for each line of credit, if the amount they borrowed stayed under the credit limit they had already been approved for.

However, many credit card customers soon wanted to be able to use their cards outside of their local area. So, in 1951, The Diners Club card was introduced, reaching thousands of cardholders very fast, and in 1958 the American Express card was created, which reached around one million cards being used in more than 85,000 establishments, not only in the U.S. but also in other countries.

These two cards technically were what we know as charge cards, meaning that their cardholders had to pay their full balance at the end of the month.

The initial credit cards were paper cards, and it was not until the 60s that they began to be issued in plastic more like current cards.

In 1970 what it's now known as Visa was created, more than a decade after what had started as the credit card BankAmericard issued by Bank of America in California. In 1979, MasterCard was created. Its beginnings were in the 60s when several California banks wanted to develop a competitor to BankAmericard, and it was initially known back then as Interbank Master Charge.

It is important to note that Visa and MasterCard don't issue cards or extend credit. They only provide to banks and other financial institutions, interchange services designed to settle credit (and debit and prepaid) card transactions, between those institutions, the merchants, and their customers all over the world.

APPENDIX B - RESOURCES

Websites

www.creditcards.com - This website provides very useful information to determine which could be the best card for your requirements. You can analyze the best options based on different factors like low rates and fees, rewards, cash back or points offered, for travel, or introductory offers. You can search by network or by the bank

www.nerdwallet.com - You will find a lot of information here that will help you choose the best options for checking; savings or money market accounts; brokers; mortgages; personal, student, or auto loans; or car or life insurance. Also, advise about budgeting, saving, and investing, among other personal finance subjects.

www.thebalance.com - On this website, you will find many good articles and useful ideas to improve your finances.

www.myfico.com/credit-education - This site demystifies credit scoring and credit reports.

www.nfcc.org - The National Foundation for Credit Counseling® (NFCC®).

www.debt.org - Here you will find useful information to control, manage and liquidate your debt.

www.bankrate.com - Loan calculators.

www.annualcreditreport.com - You can check your credit reports for free here.

www.360financialliteracy.org - In this site offered by the American Institute of CPAs, you can find information about many financial topics that you can search for, based on the different life stages you will go through.

Magazines

Kiplinger's Personal Finance - www.kiplinger.com

Books

How Money Works: THE FACTS visually explained. DK|Penguin Random House. 2017.

Cagan, Michele, and Lariviere, Elisabeth. *The Infographic Guide to Personal Finance: A Visual Reference for Everything You Need to Know*. Adams Media. 2017.

Leonard, Robin, and Loftsgordon, Amy. *Solve Your Money Troubles: Strategies to Get Out of Debt and Stay That Way*. NOLO, 2015.

NOTES

Preface

1. "The U.S. May Be the World's Richest Country, But It Ranks 14th in ...." 18 Nov. 2015, http://blogs.wsj.com/economics/2015/11/18/the-u-s-may-be-the-worlds-richest-country-but-it-ranks-14th-in-financial-literacy/.

2. The Income Quadrant

1. "Retirement Topics - Required Minimum Distributions (RMDs)." https://www.irs.gov/retirement-plans/plan-participant-employee/retirement-topics-required-minimum-distributions-rmds.

5. The Debt Quadrant

1. "Household Debt to GDP for United States© | FRED | St. Louis Fed." https://fred.stlouisfed.org/series/HDTGPDUSQ163N.
2. "Quarterly Report on Household Debt and Credit - Federal Reserve ...." https://www.newyorkfed.org/medialibrary/interactives/householdcredit/data/pdf/HHDC_2017Q3.pdf.

8. Net Worth

1. "4 Ways To Value A Real Estate Rental Property -Investopedia." http://www.investopedia.com/articles/mortgages-real-estate/11/how-to-value-real-estate-rental.asp.
2. Stanley, Thomas, J. and Danko, William, D. *The Millionaire Next Door. The Surprising Secrets of America's Wealthy*. Lanham, Maryland: Taylor Trade Publishing, 1996.

9. Debt

1. "Report on the Economic Well-Being of U.S. Households in 2016, May ...." 7

May. 2017, https://www.federalreserve.gov/publications/files/2016-report-economic-well-being-us-households-201705.pdf.

10. Why do many people overspend?

1. "38% of US Households Spend More Than Income - Shnugi." https://www.shnugi.com/2016/12/25/38-us-households-spend-earnings/.
2. "National Financial Capability Study." http://www.usfinancialcapability.org/results.php?region=US

11. How much debt is too much?

1. "American Household Credit Card Debt Statistics: 2016 - NerdWallet." 14 Dec. 2016, https://www.nerdwallet.com/blog/average-credit-card-debt-household/.

12. How to take control of your debt

1. "Research: The Best Strategy for Paying Off Credit Card Debt." 27 Dec. 2016, https://hbr.org/2016/12/research-the-best-strategy-for-paying-off-credit-card-debt.

Made in the USA
Middletown, DE
26 September 2025

18191247R00083